IN THE SHADOW
OF THE SWORDS

The Baghdad Police Academy

D. W. WILBER

CASEMATE

Philadelphia & Oxford

Published in the United States of America and Great Britain in 2020 by
CASEMATE PUBLISHERS
1950 Lawrence Road, Havertown, PA 19083, USA
and
The Old Music Hall, 106–108 Cowley Road, Oxford OX4 1JE, UK

Copyright 2020 © D. W. Wilber

Hardback Edition: ISBN 978-1-61200-921-6
Digital Edition: ISBN 978-1-61200-922-3

A CIP record for this book is available from the British Library

Printed and bound in the United States by Integrated Books International

Typeset by Versatile PreMedia Services (P) Ltd

For a complete list of Casemate titles, please contact:

CASEMATE PUBLISHERS (US)
Telephone (610) 853-9131
Fax (610) 853-9146
Email: casemate@casematepublishers.com
www.casematepublishers.com

CASEMATE PUBLISHERS (UK)
Telephone (01865) 241249
Email: casemate-uk@casematepublishers.co.uk
www.casematepublishers.co.uk

Front cover: The Crossed Swords monument in Baghdad, Iraq.

Julie, thanks for always being there
Jennifer, Lindsay and David,
thanks for putting up with your old man

Contents

Foreword

In the Shadow of the Swords will hopefully wake America up to the fact that there are dedicated men and women, not just in the military, who are working in harm's way all over the world, trying to bring a semblance of order into societies and countries that in many cases have never known it, or at least not known it for decades or even centuries. Their work is particularly important and dangerous in the many so-called 'Third World' countries that have been gripped by strife, war, or despotic and oppressive leaderships.

From the day President George W. Bush brought the War on Terror to Iraq, and up until the last American cop left the Baghdad Police Academy, men and women from law enforcement took the risks and accepted the challenges of working in a war zone to support U.S. policy and help rebuild Iraq. They dedicated themselves to improving the lives of innocent Iraqi people, yearning for a breath of freedom following the horror of life under Saddam and his regime, and the destruction brought to their historic land by an invading army.

This book looks through the eyes of the dedicated men and women who stepped up to this challenge. It also brings to light those who 'gamed' the system and literally stole money from the American taxpayer, receiving generous salaries for duties *not* performed. It shares the recollections of working with bewildered Iraqi cadets, who lacked any understanding of Western law-enforcement tactics, methods, and (especially) police ethics. It highlights the impact on family members back home, who saw the carnage on the streets of Baghdad via the daily barrage of television news, and it reveals the hypocrisy of the bureaucrats in the 'Green Zone', who attended their embassy cocktail parties and stood inside Saddam's palaces with arms folded across their chests, thinking 'deep thoughts'. Ultimately, it opens up a conversation about the wisdom of any future efforts to bring American- or Western-style law enforcement to Third World nations.

There is also plenty of humor, as seen in the daily practical jokes and camaraderie that developed between a disparate group of American (as well as some foreign) cops, thrown together in the middle of a hot war zone. You will see how we survived and faced the immense challenges of just making it through another day. Photographs paint a visual history of the places and people who were brought together and who persevered through difficult times to establish a brotherhood–in–arms, understandable only by those who answered the call.

While many books covering the challenging events of America's War on Terror have come from journalists, politicians or soldiers, not many have spoken of the effort from the viewpoint of a civilian contractor, sent to help rebuild Iraqi society following the fall of Saddam. This rebuilding included the restoration of government services, to bring back some semblance of normalcy to a society that had nearly been destroyed. As a long-time police officer and contractor in Iraq, I can tell a very different side of the story. This is not the viewpoint from the lofty towers of political appointees and senior officials, who have reputations to protect and records to defend, but rather that of someone who was on the ground, getting his hands dirty and seeing firsthand our successes and, sadly, some of our failures.

"You're making $14,000 a month and you want to complain?" Tom Burnett said to the group of instructors who approached him with questions about the weakness of the training curriculum at the Baghdad Police Academy. "I only have one thing to say, window or aisle?" This phrase, 'window or aisle', became the almost daily refrain from those running the police training program in Iraq. It signalled that they really didn't give a damn about feedback from instructors on the front lines, dealing with the challenges of actually training police cadets. All the instructors felt that six weeks of training, conducted through a translator, wasn't nearly enough, barely scratching the surface of what the cadets would need to survive on the streets of Baghdad and elsewhere in Iraq.

It is a difficult enough job on the streets of America, let alone in the extremely challenging environment of Iraq, where police were prime targets for an insurgency in full swing. But it seemed the program managers in the Green Zone were interested in only one thing—getting police officers on the streets as quickly as possible, with little regard for how well they were prepared. They were viewed as something akin to 'cannon fodder'—just toss them into the lion's den and if three-quarters of them are killed, so be it. That was the governing philosophy of the people in charge of rebuilding the Iraqi police force.

Their apparent opinion was that few knew or even cared about what was happening at an out-of-public-view training site in Baghdad, or any of the other locations around Iraq. And to be honest, most Americans simply didn't pay attention, or even know what we were doing—we didn't make the evening news. Back in the States, people were more concerned with what color to paint the spare bedroom, who to invite to next Saturday's cocktail party, or little Miss Buffy's dance recital on Tuesday night. We kicked Saddam out of Iraq, and rather quickly at that, much quicker than we had prepared for, in fact. As far as the American 'public' was concerned, what happened afterwards was someone else's problem. Those with family members in the military, or serving out there as civilians, certainly cared, but few others in America did. Nor did they really want to hear about it. We were out of sight, and easy to put out of mind.

No one knew about the American cops struggling to rebuild a police force that had been disbanded through the stupidity of American bureaucrats. Few Americans knew about people like my buddy Bob (Baghdad Boob) Manfreed, initially enticed to Iraq by the high salary, but who developed a genuine affection for the cadets he worked with each day. Not many Americans cared that instructors like my friends, and many others, were working in very basic conditions, often without even the barest necessities of life. Like toilet paper.

Instructors faced almost daily mortar attacks, as well as more simple challenges—with dozens of us packed into spaces designed for far fewer. Most Americans simply did not care that instructors had to deal with out-of-touch program managers in the Green Zone, who really didn't give a damn about us once they sent us out into the field, not even bothering to learn most of our names. These same instructors faced a constant threat of attack from within, by Iraqi cadets sympathetic to the insurgency, but no one really cared. The insurgency had developed out of the sheer stupidity exhibited by the career bureaucrats who had arrived in Iraq early after the invasion. They were the epitome of the saying, "I'm from the government and I'm here to help." There was corruption, but sadly the American public has become conditioned to it in government programs, and most accepted that at least some was inevitable. Corruption in the Iraqi Police Training Program was accepted and, sadly, far too often ignored.

But why tell the story now, with our larger involvement in Iraq 'in the rear view mirror'? With concern about radical Islamic groups like ISIS threatening to lead to a new, larger American presence in Iraq and elsewhere, the timing is ideal for a wider, deeper examination of American efforts to use civilian contractors to provide training to Third World countries. This book will remember those who sacrificed and faced the dangers in Iraq, most serving with honor and distinction when their country asked. Was this cost and risk worthwhile?

No other books have dealt with our efforts to reconstruct the Iraqi National Police following the disastrous decision by L. Paul Bremmer (the man President Bush appointed to oversee the reconstruction of Iraq) to disband the Iraqi police and start again from scratch. The dust from the collapse of Saddam's regime had barely begun to settle when a serious insurgency took root, and many of the insurgents were the same Iraqi army and police personnel who had been ousted as a result of Bremmer's decision. We are long overdue for a comprehensive narrative of American and coalition efforts to rebuild Iraqi infrastructure, of which the police are a major part.

Police officers, deputy sheriffs, federal agents, and corrections officers from all over America traveled to Iraq to answer the call for 'police trainers' to help reconstruct the Iraqi police force. Some came for the adventure, some out of a sense of patriotism, and some for no other reason than the money. Iraqi Police Trainers were indeed paid well, roughly $168,000 per year, far more than any cop would ever see back in America. Were there drawbacks? Absolutely. Living conditions were austere, and there were shortages of the basics Americans have grown accustomed to. Over in Iraq, you couldn't run down to the corner Quick Trip to pick up a roll of toilet paper or loaf of bread or gallon of milk. Aside from the separation from loved ones, there was also the constant threat of attack both from outside the academy, and from within. During one period, the academy came under daily mortar attack for over a month.

Do I sound a bit jaded and critical? You bet I do, but pointing out shortcomings in order to hopefully create a better program is the right thing to do. Since my time in Baghdad, and since I started writing this book, I'm sure there have been some improvements, and hopefully some of the waste in the program has been fixed or discarded. America still has international police-training programs going on in different parts of the world, so it's important to learn from mistakes. Hopefully, lessons will be learned.

Were we all perfect? Certainly not, no one ever is, and we made our share of mistakes. My intention is not to give a blanket indictment of everyone who oversaw the program. There was enough blame to go around, but I think the time has come for a critical look at this little-known part of the American reconstruction effort in Iraq.

About the Author

My background isn't typical for an author writing about one of the more challenging times during America's War on Terror, and the efforts in Iraq following the fall of Saddam.

I have spent a lifetime in law enforcement and intelligence-related work—as a police officer and detective for both large and small police departments in America's heartland, and as an Intelligence Officer overseas. As a published writer with credits in *S.W.A.T. Digest Magazine*, and as a columnist for Townhall.com and America Out Loud, I put into words the feelings and emotions of many of those who served under very difficult conditions. And I offer my apologies up front—this book is written in the language of cops. Cops don't talk the same as other people. Often, our experiences color our outlook on things. Those with no police experience would often view them very differently. That said, I hope I've been able to provide a coherent perspective on America's effort to help emerging democracies in the Third World, and in Iraq in particular.

I continue to work as a contractor for the U.S. government, serving in a variety of training capacities both domestically and overseas.

Acknowledgements

While there are many people to thank for their support, first and fore-most is Julie who has stuck by my side through all my overseas travels. Her daughter, Rachel, was a big help to me in getting this book ready for publication. I could go down a list of colleagues I worked with in Baghdad, but think I'll just say a collective 'thank you' to all of those who answered the call.

All characters mentioned in the book are based on real people, or composites of those I worked with. I offer only my perspective as that of others may differ. And all names have been changed.

Introduction

In the Shadow of the Swords has been over a decade in the making, with plenty of starts and stops, as well as some detours along the way, including the occasional 'what the hell, let's just drop this whole thing.' America's effort in Iraq lasted through the presidency of George W. Bush and ended during the presidency of his successor, Barack H. Obama. Legitimate arguments can be made on whether or not we should have ever gone into Iraq. While I dismiss those who chant 'Bush Lied and People Died' as nothing more than political hacks, I will give credence to the more thoughtful who argue that mistakes were made and the war could have been better prosecuted. Indeed, mistakes were made, the most egregious in my mind coming early on, when the decision was made that anyone with any connection to the previous regime's Baathist Party would not be welcome in the new Iraqi police and military forces. This decision helped provide the budding insurgency with a cadre of experienced fighters, who later killed and maimed thousands of members of the U.S. military, other coalition forces, civilian government employees, and private contractors working in Iraq.

The well-publicized 'surge', which came much later, created the possibility of Iraq emerging from decades of brutality and war, and becoming a valued partner in the Middle East. Iraq was on the right path, but in my opinion the Obama administration's policies and strategies in dealing with the Iraqi leadership led that country back to the brink of dissolution, with the potential for Iraq to fall into chaos and anarchy following the rise of the Islamic State. This is without even mentioning the Islamic Republic of Iran asserting control over Iraq, its adversary in a decade-long war that had killed over half a million from both sides.

Finally, I should mention that it was a privilege for me to work alongside some of the finest people from American law enforcement that I have ever encountered. Most I have lost touch with, but there are still a few with whom I have kept an open line of communication. Sadly, some are no longer with us, like Bob Manfreed, my brother from another mother who I lost suddenly several years ago. Not a day goes by that I don't recall him with fondness. I miss you Brother, but I'll see you on the other side. Keep the cooler full and iced down!

CHAPTER I

There's a Hell of a Gunfight Going On

The sounds of gunfire outside the compound, several hundred yards off, caught our attention as we sat around the fire pit chatting with each other. Our evening ritual, our version of a 'choir practice', had already begun even though it was only around four in the afternoon. I looked over at Rick and Tracy and joked, "Hope to hell that's not Two Dogs and Bob's convoy getting hit. Wouldn't that be a trip?" The gunfire lasted for roughly a minute or two and then came to an abrupt end with one final, long burst of automatic weapons fire. With the excitement over, we returned to our conversation, which likely had to do with either the day's events while teaching the Iraqi cadets, or discussing new ideas for maintaining a steady supply of alcohol deliveries to the academy. As well as the obligatory 'war stories' shared from our police careers.

Hearing gunfire wasn't all that unusual in Baghdad, since everybody had an AK-47 in the home. Not to mention RPGs (Rocket Propelled Grenades) and many other weapons and explosive devices. It was always worse on Thursdays, which was the day Iraqis typically tied the proverbial knot. The wedding ceremony would be followed by a feast or reception, which always included a great deal of gunfire, with the men shooting their rifles and pistols into the air in celebration.

This was not the kind of thing Americans were used to—even a 'shotgun wedding' wouldn't usually result in the weapon actually being discharged. This sort of gunfire was therefore referred to as 'happy fire', and it wasn't limited to wedding celebrations. Sometimes the locals would just get the urge during an evening to step out onto the front porch and fire into the air for no apparent reason.

The first time anyone experiences a Thursday in Baghdad, their automatic reaction is to be concerned and maybe even start ducking for cover, only to realize that they are the only ones hiding. Everyone else, the old timers 'in country' who know the deal, just continue with whatever they are doing. Then the newcomer will sheepishly get back up from the ground, or from behind the barricade where they had sought cover. This is usually followed by some good-natured ridicule from those who have seen it all before, and who once did the same thing when they were new to Iraq. Now, an actual ambush or attack on a Thursday can be a confusing event for sure. Is someone getting married, or are you getting your ass shot at? It is disconcerting to say the least.

Jimmy 'Two Dogs' and 'Baghdad Boob' had gone to the Green Zone earlier in the day to interview for one of the many admin jobs that came up regularly, either over in the Green Zone itself or at other academies around the country. Such jobs were almost always were filled by 'insiders', who had been in a position to brown-nose the decision makers. One thing we quickly learned was that merit or qualifications mattered little with the ICITAP program in Iraq (International Criminal Investigation Training Assistance Program—someone must have been paid quite a bit to come up with that moniker.) In Baghdad's Green Zone it was all about who you knew, and who you blew. Those who got there first were able to stake a claim to many of the positions available in the relative comfort and safety of the Green Zone, along with all the additional 'palace perks' that came with it—Saddam's Palace swimming pool, the PX (Post Exchange, a shop for military personnel), more freedom of movement in a fairly secure zone, the availability of alcohol, and *women*. Of course, the competition for available women was stiff indeed, with senior military officers, diplomats, and other higher-level government types leading the charge to try to score with the relatively small number of women serving there (relationships with Iraqi women were strongly discouraged).

The interview process for jobs in the Green Zone was a matter of going through the motions, since decisions on who was getting what position had almost always been made long before. Being based in the Green

Zone, where you could curry favor with the bosses, was a prerequisite, and if you weren't willing to kiss a little ass, then your chances of landing a cushy job were pretty slim. It was a very cliquish environment.

So why would someone risk a convoy ride into the Green Zone and interview for a job they knew they had no chance of getting, and very likely didn't even want? That is easy to explain. While interviewing, you almost always had to stay overnight in the tent at the Adnan Palace, where the 'Baghdad County Club' was located. From there, you would be able to visit the big PX, along with the vendors stationed right outside it, as well as the local shops and cafés, where alcohol could be purchased. There were even a few places to eat, including a Chinese restaurant, but this wasn't very tempting—dogs and cats ran free all over Baghdad, except around the Chinese restaurant in the Green Zone.

There had once been another restaurant, not too far from the PX, called the Green Zone Café, where lots of Americans and other coalition personnel often gathered. There was also a local vendor area, where Iraqis could sell their wares—both places ended up being attacked by suicide bombers and quite a few people, including several Americans, were killed in the attacks. The Green Zone Café never reopened and the vendor area was also closed down.

The PX in the Green Zone was a short walk across a couple of streets and parking lots near Saddam's former palace, which was being used by the military and government as our embassy and headquarters at the time. Saddam's palace was a huge building, which at one time had huge statues of his head atop its four corners. The PX wasn't particularly large by American standards, but it sufficed to meet the needs of those serving in the Green Zone, or those passing through who wanted to pick up a souvenir t-shirt. There were many t-shirts, as well as junk food, other clothing, canned goods, and even electronics like large flat-screen TVs. Right outside the PX one could also buy items unique to Iraq from local vendors—unit or specialized 'challenge coins', military-style shoulder or vest patches of all types, t-shirts with catchy little Iraqi or military slogans. There was a coffee shop and a Burger King there as well, or you could just take a seat and people watch, which was always a fun thing to do in the Green Zone.

It was fun to sit there and pick out the various PSD (Protective Security Detail) outfits operating in Baghdad. They all wore cargo pants and OD (Olive Drab) green t-shirts, allowing their bulging muscles to be on display, along with multiple tattoos and full beards or goatees. Close-cut hair was the norm, or maybe an OD green baseball cap with the subdued American flag on the front, and Oakley sunglasses propped above the eyes or hanging off the back of the head. Each would be carrying the obligatory 9mm pistol, holstered low on the thigh, along with an M-4 or AK-47 hanging from a shoulder. Blackwater was the most well-known (some might say notorious) PSD operating in theater, but there were quite a few others as well.

For those who don't know what a PSD is, it's basically an up-armored SUV convoy, which careened around the streets of Baghdad, terrorizing Baghdad commuters and even pedestrians. One never knew when they might just decide to drive right up onto a sidewalk to avoid a traffic jam. Staffed by heavily armed men with lots of tattoos, tactical vests stocked with magazines, and wearing the unofficial Iraqi contractor 'uniform' already described, most PSD teams were made up of former military personnel, heavy on special operations and infantry types. There were even some South Africans thrown into the mix, but most were Americans who had left the military after their enlistments ended in order to cash in on the big money being paid to PSDers, escorting people and officials around Baghdad outside the Green Zone. They were often referred to as 'gunslingers', and there were a number of serious incidents involving PSD units in Iraq, most notably the one in which a Blackwater unit shot up a street full of Iraqis, killing and wounding quite a few, for which the unit was later brought up on charges. Blackwater was the main company operating inside Iraq, providing PSD services to many U.S. government officials, including diplomats and CIA case officers, who needed to move around the city to conduct business.

The convoys, usually made up of four or five SUVs, raced around the city streets pushing innocent local cars out of the way, busting through intersections, blowing their horns, and occasionally firing a warning shot at any Iraqi vehicle that drove too close. Large signs printed in English and Arabic on the back of each vehicle usually said something to the effect of 'Stay back 100 feet, if you don't we'll kill you'—a pretty clear message to anyone that approaching close to a PSD was a mistake. They were also called 'bullet magnets', because they stood out like a sore thumb among the typical Iraqi vehicles on the streets, and often were ambushed by insurgents and Al-Qaeda in Iraq fighters. Probably a few off-duty Iraqi police and army members took pot shots at them now and then too. Some creative PSD companies had the idea of using vehicles that were painted like Iraqi taxi cabs—a white body with orange-painted front and rear fenders. Less noticeable, they blended in better with the typical Iraqi traffic and had a fair level of success at avoiding getting the hell shot out of them.

Every Iraqi bad guy knew when they saw a PSD convoy barreling towards them that it was a target of opportunity. Perhaps the convoy was ferrying an American diplomat or general, or maybe even a CIA officer on his way to meet with an Iraqi who had infiltrated the insurgency. Each would be a feather in the cap of any Iraqi who could kill them. Whatever the reason for the PSD convoy's presence, they made easy targets for the bad guys to identify and shoot at, or attack with an IED.

In addition to visiting the PX and people-watching, trips to the Green Zone also afforded the opportunity to make a 'tactical beer run' to the Napoli Café and pick up supplies to last you until the next person interviewed for some non-existent job. There were other places in the Green Zone where you could pick up alcohol, but the Café Napoli usually had a pretty fair selection, for hard liquor anyway. With beer it was always 'take what you can get'. Corona was usually available, along with Amstel. On one visit I picked up a case of Heineken that had a logo on the can celebrating the soccer World Cup from about 10 years earlier. Obviously it had been sitting somewhere, 'aging', for a long time.

That's why Baghdad Boob and Two Dogs had decided to apply and interview for one of the openings, simply to get a ride to the Green Zone, shop the PX, and stock up on booze and other adult beverages. The fact that they could get killed in an ambush or by an IED didn't faze them, or indeed any of us who were willing to make the trip. It was a nice diversion from the monotony of the Baghdad Academy, and anyone going to the Green Zone always took special orders from their colleagues as well. Oftentimes the up-armored SUVs came back the next day fully loaded with cases of beer and bottles of booze. Not that anyone serving at the Baghdad Academy was a raving drunk or alcoholic—you just didn't know when you might have another opportunity to have some alcohol on hand for a quiet evening drink around the fire pit, so you always took advantage of a trip to the Green Zone and loaded up.

After the sound of gunfire had interrupted our evening by the fire pit, the calm was further shattered by the PSD convoy rolling into the inner academy compound, throwing dirt and gravel around as it came to an abrupt stop. Immediately we noticed a large number of bullet holes in the exterior skins of the SUVs that made up the four-vehicle convoy. We didn't know if they were new holes, or old ones that had never been repaired. The doors popped open and out stepped the convoy team and two very familiar faces, Jimmy Two Dogs and Baghdad Boob, both smiling somewhat sheepishly. They shook hands with the PSD team and then still wearing their full 'battle rattle' (Kevlar helmets and body armor with front strike plate), they walked casually over to the fire pit. Two Dogs spoke first. "Did you hear the shooting?" he asked. We looked at them curiously as Bob added, "That was us, we got ambushed coming back from the Green Zone." We all looked at them quizzically. Then, not wanting to exhibit any concern in front of them, I asked, "Did you guys get the booze?" As far as they knew, all we cared about was whether or not they had completed their mission, which was to conduct a tactical beer run and obtain the necessary supplies. To show any concern about them personally would not have been 'manly'.

After assuring us that the cargo was safely inside the PSD vehicles, waiting to be unloaded, Bob went on to describe in detail what had happened. This was the very first, real-life, actual ambush any of our group (who had all come over to Baghdad together) had been involved in, so we were keyed up and interested in hearing the details. Unfortunately, there would be more such incidents and other attacks. According to Bob, they had been approaching a well-known traffic roundabout not too far from the academy entrance—maybe several hundred yards away—when they had run into a traffic jam and their PSD had to come to a stop. All at once automatic weapons had opened up on them from Iraqi insurgents on the nearby rooftops. The SUVs had been riddled with bullet holes but fortunately for the PSD occupants the armor had held—for a while anyway. The driver of Jimmy and Bob's vehicle had yelled into the radio, communicating with the lead SUV, "Punch a hole through, we're getting shot to hell just sitting here!" The armor used in the SUVs had a limited life-span, as with the bullet-resistant glass, and would eventually fail if they didn't get out of the kill zone fairly quickly.

According to Bob, a vehicle suddenly started to approach the convoy from a side street. One of the PSD 'shooters' shouted, "I think we got a VBIED (Vehicle Borne Improvised Explosive Device—the military loved acronyms) headed our way!", and he fired a warning burst towards the vehicle, trying to get it to stop heading in their direction. They could see only one occupant, the male Iraqi driver as he continued to drive towards the convoy, refusing to stop and ignoring the warning shots. A few seconds later the PSD shooter fired off another burst directly at the vehicle engine but it continued moving towards the stalled convoy. With all the other gunfire still hitting the convoy, everyone was beginning to get a little concerned. As the Iraqi vehicle continued to approach the convoy, the PSD shooter leaned out the back of his SUV and fired a long burst, right at the driver. The inside of the vehicle's windshield exploded in crimson and the vehicle rolled to a stop. "Threat gone," the shooter said as he turned his attention back to the rooftops.

The gunfire continued to come at them, so the lead vehicle began to push Iraqi cars out of the way, making an opening the rest of the convoy could pass through, as Iraqi drivers yelled and shook their fists at them. Finally the AK-47 fire tapered off as the convoy drove clear of the 'kill zone'.

"We thought the car was a suicide bomber since he wouldn't stop and kept approaching," said Bob. "Hopefully it wasn't just some Iraqi dude running late to his kid's birthday party. Oops."

Jimmy Two Dogs added, "Sounded like the worst hail storm I've ever been in my whole life. I had one round hit the window right next to my head and the frigging glass just spider-webbed. Fortunately it was bullet-resistant, or the inside of my window would have turned crimson like with that car heading towards us. And the seat of my cargo pants would have turned a very dark brown."

I looked up at Bob from my chair and said, "Good story Bob, did you get any beer?"

Thus began the legend of Two Dogs and Baghdad Boob being awarded the 'Loyal Order of the Crappy Pants'. An achievement not exactly coveted, but certainly recognized and respected by all.

CHAPTER 2

Our Introduction to ICITAP

The Comfort Inn, in Lorton, Virginia, was where we all met for the first time. It was October of 2004 and there were 20 of us 'contractors' going over to Iraq together to serve as International Police Trainers for the Iraqi police. Our travel to Virginia was the initial step in the process we all had to complete as part of our eventual movement over to Iraq. The contracting agency had arranged for our lodging at a small hotel in Lorton. We had joined the program for a variety of reasons, and we all possessed a law-enforcement background, either as commissioned police officers or, in some cases, as corrections officers. Supposedly, this was a prerequisite for acceptance into the program, but we would find out later that wasn't necessarily the truth. Sometimes it was who you knew at the contracting company that mattered, and this policy ultimately made for some interesting relationships and situations at the academy.

Lots of people were interested in the high salaries being paid and if they could finagle their way into the program, they would. That's more or less the origin of the 'window or aisle' threat. By this time word had gotten out about the money and there were many people interested in taking your place in the program.

We came from small towns, larger ones, municipal police departments from big cities, or county sheriff positions. There were even some people from federal agencies like the FBI, DEA, U.S. Customs, and Border Patrol. At least initially for most of us, the lure of big money had brought us to this point. In order to get law-enforcement professionals to join the project and take the risks of going to a war zone in Iraq, the Department of Justice had to offer high salaries, much higher than any of us would have dreamed of making as a police officer back in the United States. Police work has never been noted for making one wealthy—at least not honestly anyway! The pay came out to just over $13,000 per month, plus a *per diem*. Not bad at all, as someone from a small-town police department may have earned just $15,000 per year.

Some had come to help pay for their kids' college fees, to pay off a mortgage, or to buy a vacation property or retirement home somewhere. The big money was definitely the lure that attracted many, if not most, to the program. Others came because, as is not uncommon among cops, they had found themselves with huge debts and money problems from multiple divorces and child support. And in many cases it was simply the boredom of retirement. After being a cop for many years, some people find it difficult to retire and do nothing. I've worked with officers who retired after spending 25 or 30 years with one department, then took another cop job on a college campus or something like that. Oftentimes it was a matter of finances—a cop's pension doesn't always cover the bills, much like military veterans who retire and then go to work for the federal government in order to 'double dip'.

Each of us had accepted the challenges of going to Iraq in the hopes that the payoff would outweigh the risks. None of us had a death wish, but we all knew in the back of our minds that there was a chance we might not come back home, at least not in one piece. I mean, after all, it was a freaking war zone. People were getting blown up, shot, and having their heads cut off for cripe's sake! It was a much more intense environment than most of us had ever experienced during our careers as police officers. As law-enforcement professionals, we faced the reality every day that we might not come home at the end of our shift, as did our families and loved ones. Each day that you left your home, you knew in the back of your mind that there was a chance you might get killed by some crazed lunatic or criminal. It was a reality each officer faced in different ways. But working in the war zone of Iraq was different.

Truthfully, most police officers go through their whole career never drawing their weapon or engaging in a shoot-out with a bad guy, let alone getting wounded or killed in the line of duty. What you see on television is fantasy, just make-believe. Yes, it is potentially a dangerous profession, but the shoot-outs depicted in the movies are a rarity. Police are trained to deescalate situations before they reach the need for deadly force, and most of the time they're pretty successful at bringing some difficult, even dangerous situation to a conclusion without the need for gunplay.

Certainly we all hoped we wouldn't get blown up in Iraq. We all hoped that we would return home after a year or so, healthy, wealthy, and wiser for the experience. Some of us did, and some of us didn't. One of our group actually returned home more in debt than when he left! His wife—now ex-wife—emptied out their joint bank account, maxed out the credit cards, and disappeared with all the money he made in Iraq. For the most part, though, we enhanced our financial situation, and I certainly left a wiser man than I was when I first went over to Baghdad. My feelings about the Iraqi people had changed, as well as my feelings about my government's involvement in their country.

Being thrown in together as strangers, we all had at least one thing in common—our experiences in law enforcement, which helped to break the ice during our first gathering at the hotel in Lorton. Cops always have 'war stories' to tell each other, only in this case we would eventually all have real war stories from our experiences in Iraq. As the old joke goes, 'Do you know the difference between a fairy tale and a war story? A fairy tale starts out "Once upon a time", and a war story starts out "This ain't no shit".' Most police war stories are at least based on an element of truth, but oftentimes there is also some level of embellishment involved, and usually a great deal of humor, that gallows humor I've already mentioned and that you hear about often among the police. What might be a life-and-death situation, or something very tragic, often becomes a funny story that officers can laugh about later. It's part of the coping mechanism cops use to deal with those types of things. It helps them keep their sanity. That first evening, as we stood around and chatted, there were more than a few war stories shared among us newfound friends, friends who eventually would become a band of brothers.

One of the first people I got to know among my new group of colleagues was Roy, who had served as a homicide detective for a large police department in Arizona. He seemed to be a genuinely decent guy, a real family man. He was friendly and outgoing and spoke a lot about his two sons back home. He was already missing them and we hadn't even left the United States yet. Another, named Dalma, had risen to a senior level with the U.S. Border Patrol prior to retiring. And then there was Jimmy (later renamed 'Two Dogs') who was retired from the U.S. Customs Service. His eventual roommate at the academy, Bob (later renamed 'Baghdad Boob') was a retired IRS Special Agent. We also had Stan and Ruby, a husband-and-wife team who had signed on together from a county sheriff's department in Georgia, along with Kenny, a colleague of theirs from their earlier lives as Georgia police officers. I had signed on following a dozen years of service as a police officer and detective in the St. Louis area. The sheer breadth of experience among us was pretty amazing. The program had former DEA and FBI special agents, county sheriff deputies, senior level corrections officers, major metropolitan police officers, and small-town cops.

I had served in uniform patrol as a police officer, where I had been involved in one shooting scrape (where I came out on top), and plenty of other wrestling matches with bad guys. This was followed by a stint as an under-cover detective with a narcotics unit, and my last few years were spent as an investigator with the major case squad, where I worked on a number of high-profile homicide investigations. I received about a dozen commendations over the years and was fairly proud of the job I had done in my career up to that point.

Oftentimes, police officers can become jaded by their exposure to the seamier side of society, as well as the tragedies they see every day, but I have to say that one of the highlights of my career happened one sunny weekend, when something occurred that made everything I had done as a police officer worthwhile. I had stopped at a 7-11 to grab a cup of coffee and was headed back out to my squad car. Next to my car was a large white SUV, and seated in the front passenger seat was a little white-haired old lady, to whom I'd paid little notice as I started to enter my car.

It was a really nice day outside and she had the window of her vehicle open. All of a sudden I heard, "Excuse me, officer." Right away,

I expected to be asked for directions to some place or whatever, as often happens to police officers. People also sometimes want to talk to you to complain, or to just make a connection. I put my coffee down on top of my car and turned around to see what the lady wanted. I got my first real glimpse of this sweet little old lady, who proceeded to say, "I know you all have a really tough job, and you don't hear much praise, mostly complaints from people. I just wanted to tell you, thank you, I appreciate what you do for us." I was stunned, it was not at all what I expected to hear. I looked at the lady—probably with disbelief on my face—and I thanked her for her kind words. I told her that I was going to share her comments with my co-workers, and that she had made my day.

I then got into my squad car and drove off, determined to take as many bad guys off the streets as I could to make the world a little bit safer for that little old white-haired lady. And I did go back to the police station and share her comments with all of the officers I was working with that day. I don't know if it meant anything to them, but it sure did to me, and after all these years and miles I still get misty-eyed when I think of that sweet little lady's kindness. As far as I'm concerned, that was the highlight of my police career.

During our first evening together in Virginia, we all gathered in the hotel lobby waiting for an orientation meeting that was set to begin around six o'clock. A representative from the contracting company (his name long since forgotten), began our first meeting in a small room off from the lobby.

"Don't even think about having your family use me as a point of contact," he started off. He provided us a business card with his name, title, and contact information printed on the front, and then informed us that he didn't want to be receiving phone calls from our family members with messages to pass on, emergencies to notify us about, or for any other reason. There would be other avenues to do that. During a break in the briefing, while he took a phone call, the consensus among our group was that he was a huge pompous ass. Following the meeting, in conversations among ourselves, many of us decided then and there to pass his information to our families and have them put his name at the top of their list of contacts in the event of an emergency, or even if a question came up. He was a real dickhead.

During the meeting, he also tried to regale us with stories of his previous overseas experiences as part of the ICITAP program in Haiti, where he had served for a short period of time in some capacity. Just based on his attitude alone we were all mightily unimpressed. It was later determined that the company he represented was being replaced in the near future and was no longer going to be involved in the ICITAP program, which I guess is what prompted his poor attitude, but he was still a real jerk about it. At least that was the consensus of everyone in our group after the briefing, and even though his company would be leaving the program, I still gave his contact information to my family, encouraging them to call him with any questions, as did most of the others from our group.

Our agenda for the next few days was also laid out during this meeting. The representative told us that it would start the next morning with a trip to downtown Washington, D.C., where we would spend the day with the Justice Department for briefings and paperwork. The following day there would be a trip into the Virginia countryside to 'the Crucible', a weapons and tactics training area run by another government contractor, where we would receive some weapons familiarization and get issued with equipment. On the next day we would be sent to Fort Belvoir, Virginia, for medical processing and to obtain our official government ID card, which would give us access to U.S. military facilities in Iraq. Following that, we would be booked on a commercial flight and depart the United States on the first leg of our trip to Iraq, by way of Kuwait City. While I can remember very little else from this initial meeting, I do recall that all of us walked out of there with the same feeling. What in the hell did we get ourselves into?

After adjourning from the meeting with the forgettable contracting representative, some of our group, whose wives had accompanied them to Virginia, headed out to dinner. Others went back to their hotel rooms to relax, and some just lingered around the lobby area and engaged in casual conversation with their new friends. After briefly chatting in the lobby, and never once saying 'this ain't no shit' to anyone, I walked over to the elevator and took it up one floor to my room. As I exited the elevator and began to walk down the hallway, I noticed a guest room door propped wide open. Inside, I recognized one of my new colleagues, Jimmy, who was smoking a cigar and drinking a can of beer.

Jimmy was drinking a can of Miller Light from a six-pack he had sitting on ice in the sink of his bathroom. Being a St. Louis boy, the home of Anheuser Busch, I decided to overlook his poor taste in beer and stepped in to formally introduce myself.

"How's it going, I'm Del," I said.

Jimmy was busy fiddling with his laptop computer, trying to tap into a nearby wireless signal, which he had discovered emanating from some nearby residence. The hotel had a wireless service available but charged for it, and Jimmy was looking for a way to avoid paying the fee. I pulled up a chair and sat down and we began to chat.

"Piece of crap computer," Jimmy cursed as I sat down. I discovered during our conversation that Jimmy was a retired U.S. Customs Agent and had worked narcotics cases over the last several years of his career. He was also fluent in Spanish. I also found out that he loved to smoke those nasty cigars that looked like a piece of a branch or twig from a tree—all twisted and gnarled. They smelled really, really bad, too. I had quit smoking cigarettes quite a few years earlier, but occasionally still enjoyed toying with a fine cigar. I made a mental note to work on improving Jimmy's taste in cigars as well as beer.

Jimmy and I exchanged biographies while we sat together and drank a few beers. I had also put a six-pack on ice (I had opted for an Anheuser Busch product, naturally), and since my room was nearby I walked down and retrieved one, and then returned to visit more with Jimmy.

"So what did you think of the orientation?" Jimmy asked.

I responded, "I thought the asshole running the meeting was a dickhead."

Jimmy made it clear that he was inclined to agree, adding, "I'm going to make sure my wife gets his name and phone number, with instructions to call him at least once a day just to screw with him."

"Sounds like a plan to me,' I said. "I'm going to do the same."

We had a pleasant conversation and it was obvious that Jimmy was an easy-going, good-natured guy. He certainly wasn't a stick in the mud, nor all caught up with himself as some police officers have been known to be (unfortunately we would find that tendency was common within the Iraqi police program once we reached Baghdad).

While Jimmy and I were chatting, some of the others of our group wandered by the open door, some stopping by briefly to chat, others just waving at us as they walked by. Across the hallway from Jimmy was another member of our group named Ted. Ted would later be tagged with the nickname of 'Tackleberry', taken from the *Police Academy* series of movies. Ted came with three duffle bags full of his own 'tactical' gear. This was in addition to his regular luggage, and I found out later that he possessed by far the largest collection of pornography of any one person I have ever known.

I recall Roy from Arizona telling me the story of his first meeting with Ted while we were at the hotel in Lorton. Roy is a fairly religious person, a good family man, and pretty much what you would call a 'straight arrow'. According to Roy, he was walking past the open door of Ted's room when Ted recognized him and called out, "Hey you gotta see this!", sounding all excited. Recognizing Ted as part of our group, Roy stepped into his room, only to be 'treated' to some form of disgusting pornography that Ted was playing on the TV in his room. Being a decent guy and not one to cause confrontations, Roy didn't make a scene, but quickly excused himself and stepped back outside. As he related the story he kind of chuckled about the fact that Ted didn't know him in the slightest, yet invited him right into his room to partake of his pornographic offering. Roy seemed more amused than offended, saying, "I'm not really sure about that guy," as he walked away.

Ted also decided to break away from his entertainment and stop by to chat briefly with Jimmy and I. He had noticed that Jimmy had located a strong wireless internet signal and was trying to tap into it to check his e-mail.

"Any luck with the wireless?" he asked. In addition to his bags of tactical gear, Ted brought with him a kind of 'Jack-of-all-trades' ability, which came in handy once we reached Baghdad. We would later joke that Ted knew just enough about all types of subjects to make himself somewhat dangerous.

Ted joined our attempts to tap into the signal, but I don't think we were ever were able to get it to work. It was probably password-protected anyway, but it did help to kill some time and gave Jimmy and me a reason to drink a couple of beers together as we worked diligently on the problem. Eventually Jimmy said "fuck it," and we decided to call it a night.

When I returned to my room, I had a sense that this might not be such a bad gig after all, as long as I stayed alive. Jimmy seemed like someone I would be able to get along with, and Roy was also a decent guy, so it looked like there would be at least a couple of people that I could hang with once we got over to Iraq.

The next morning our group loaded into vans provided by the contracting company and left our hotel to attend the briefings at the Department of Justice in downtown Washington, D.C. Most of our group had never been to D.C. before, and they looked out the windows at the monuments and museums as we cut our path through the traffic to get to our destination. I had lived in the area for two years during an earlier life and had seen it all, so I tried to catch up on some of the sleep I'd missed out on the night before, since I don't do well sleeping in hotel rooms.

Upon arrival at the Department of Justice, where our orientation was to take place, we entered through a security checkpoint and were ushered up several floors to a medium-sized classroom. Once there, we were introduced to some representatives from the department, and after completing some paperwork and reviewing some documents, our briefing sessions began.

The fact that I remember very little from this full day of briefings testifies to the impact the disseminated information had on all of us. I'm pretty confident that none of our group derived much of value or anything really memorable from this day. The briefings were dry and not very informative, and the briefers weren't stellar performers.

I was not the only one who expressed the opinion that what we had just endured was pretty much a waste of all our time. We would have done better to partake of the cultural offerings of downtown D.C., enjoying the museums and monuments (or strip clubs), rather than sitting in a classroom being lectured by some nameless government bureaucrat.

One thing I do recall from that day was that a professor from American University gave us a lecture about Arab culture and sensibilities. But it certainly didn't register with most of us and the majority of his comments were quickly forgotten or dismissed. One comment of note, though, was a warning to avoid any romantic relationships with Iraqi women. That was apparently frowned upon by Iraqi men and could get both you *and her* killed. The day fortunately came to an end and we were once again loaded into the vans for our drive through the D.C. rush-hour traffic.

Back at the hotel, my evening shaped up pretty much like the one before—sitting in Jimmy's room, having a beer or two, smelling his nasty cigars, and trying to tap into the wireless internet signal for a couple of hours. I recall nothing of earth-shattering significance occurring during the evening and once again, after the beer ran out and I could stand no more of Jimmy's cigars, I eventually made my way back to my own room and to bed. And once again I had a fitful night of sleep. I'm not sure whether it was the excitement of what lay ahead that kept me awake, or whether it was apprehension, knowing that within another couple of days we all would be on our way to Iraq.

Our agenda for the next day included a trip to the Crucible, where we would receive some hands-on familiarization and training with weapons. Since all of us came from a law-enforcement background, this would be viewed as a 'mental health day', where we would get some good trigger-time in on the government's nickel. Cops love to shoot, and this day would be no exception—we would receive familiarization with an AK-47, which many of us had never handled or fired before. That proved to be a treat, and anytime you get cops and guns together for some shooting at someone else's expense, it's a great day.

The next morning we again loaded into the vans for an hour's drive to the Crucible, which was in the countryside outside of town. None of us really knew what to expect, as our briefings from the first evening at the hotel hadn't gone into much detail. When we arrived we were greeted by some instructors and led into a building, where there was a large classroom. We took seats at the tables that were laid out in rows.

On the tables were AK-47 rifles, M-4 carbines (which are carried by the U.S. military in Iraq), and 9mm semi-automatic pistols, which most of us were familiar with from our law-enforcement careers. The lead instructor, who (we were told) was a former Chilean commando and whose physical presence was imposing, oversaw our classroom briefings and training.

During the morning we were given some basic weapon-safety briefings and some hands-on handling of the M-4 Carbine, the Beretta 9mm pistol, and the Kalishnikov AK-47 assault rifle. While I had some experience with an AK-47, most of my colleagues had never seen one up close before. We spent some time breaking down the weapons and putting them back together, which most of us were able to do with little difficulty since we had handled weapons for most of our lives.

Following lunch, we walked a short distance from the classroom to a nearby outdoor firing range. Being out in the Virginia countryside, we were surrounded by hills and forests and there were no visible structures anywhere around, other than the classroom building and a couple of other small buildings associated with this facility. We were instructed to pre-load magazines for each weapon to be fired. After getting all the magazines loaded, we were broken down into small groups and instructed to move up to the firing line.

As a part of our familiarization with the weapons, we were allowed to fire one magazine of ammunition from each one, aiming at paper targets approximately 25 yards away. Throughout the morning we could hear small-arms fire and even small explosions a short distance away, in the wooded areas surrounding the classroom buildings. We were told that some other unidentified groups were at the facility, receiving some advanced tactical and other weapon and combat-related training. It was never confirmed but we suspected it was some kind of 'spook' training that was going on around us. A number of small explosions also occurred while we were at the range so it was obvious that our small-arms training wasn't the only thing going on in the Virginia countryside that day.

Some of us shot much better than others, and some were downright scary handling a weapon, especially Dudley, who came to be known as 'the Pillsbury Dough Boy'. His handling of weapons didn't engender any peace of mind for those who stood around him on the firing line.

After we finished, we all gathered around a table to clean and service the weapons we had just fired. Everyone had thoroughly enjoyed themselves, as would be expected of a bunch of cops. It's always fun shooting up someone else's ammunition, and the only downside was that we didn't get to shoot more than one magazine for each weapon. Most of us would have been content to spend the whole day shooting.

Following this, we proceeded to another building, where we were to receive a supply of clothing and equipment that would accompany us along with our personal luggage to Iraq. Body armor vests, helmets, tactical web-gear, cold-weather clothes, boots, sleeping bags, and some nice khaki cargo pants and shirts were issued to us. It could have easily filled four duffle bags, but we had to stuff it all into two. The gear we received was all top-dollar stuff, and while I don't know the exact amount Uncle Sam paid for all of it, suffice it to say that we were each outfitted with probably a couple of thousand dollars' worth of gear, at least (our boy 'Tackleberry' was on cloud nine). I couldn't help but think of the scene from the movie *Stripes*, when Bill Murray was getting issued all of his military uniforms and made the comment that, "Chicks in New York are paying top dollar for this crap."

After a great deal of struggle—packing, un-packing, and then re-packing the gear we had just been issued—most of us were able to stuff the duffle bags full and actually get them closed. It took me two tries to get everything to fit inside my bags, but I was finally able to get it all inside. Some of the others of our group never did get all their gear jammed in. They ended up carrying their helmets or other pieces of gear loose, outside the duffle bags, until they got back to the hotel, where they could try again.

All of the clothing and equipment that we received was top quality—511 cargo pants and shirts, as well as cold-weather clothing, and all of it we got to keep, with the exception of the protective gear like the Kevlar helmets and body armor with strike plates. That gear we had to turn back in when we left Iraq.

Once back at the hotel, my first thoughts were that I was going to have to get rid of some of the stuff I had brought with me from Missouri, or I would never be able to carry everything to Iraq. I was in a quandary. Having been to Iraq previously, on a different job, I had a pretty good idea of what was needed and what was wanted over there, and I had packed my personal luggage accordingly. Now I had two more duffle bags to lug around once I made it to Baghdad. I certainly didn't want to give up any of my personal belongings, but I knew I had to accommodate this new load and figure out a way to get it all over there. There weren't going to be any airport Sky Caps over in Baghdad to help with the luggage, so a few of us decided to look for some sort of luggage cart to bring with us.

Several of us loaded up into a van and went to a nearby Walmart on a cart-buying mission. I found a nice, sturdy luggage cart for $25 and purchased it right away. It looked as though it would handle my duffle bags and the other 'drag bag' I had brought from home. I'd have to carry my laptop and wear a backpack separately. The others were also able to find something comparable, so we all checked out and headed back to the hotel.

Once back, the evening shaped up as a replay of the previous ones— meeting in Jimmy's room, having a couple beers, trying to tap into a wireless signal, and then going to bed. Since the next day brought our medical processing, I decided to take it easy on the beer. I didn't want my blood to appear yellow in the vial when they took a sample.

The next morning we again loaded into vans and drove to Fort Belvoir, where we obtained our Department of Defense CAC cards. The CAC (Common Access Card) is the identification used to gain access to military and government facilities in Iraq and elsewhere. The civilian government rank that was put on the cards identified us all as a GS-15 (equivalent), which equated in the military to something along the lines of a full colonel or brigadier general. Apparently, after numerous complaints from *real* generals and *real* GS-15s, the practice of assigning a high government rank to CAC cards for contractors was later abolished. I heard there were some abuses mixed in there somewhere, by civilian contractors who tried to use the GS-15 rank for extra perks over in

Iraq or during travel on military flights. That seemed likely—if you give anyone a chance, they'll try to game the system for their benefit.

Our medical processing was also completed at the same location. The males of our group had the distinct pleasure of being examined by a young and very attractive female doctor. She was a doll and I know that all of us fell in love with her on the spot. There was much conversation among the men and hopes were high that she would check us all for hernias. Unfortunately, none of us were asked to drop trousers, turn our head to the side and cough. It would have been the highlight of the day for most of us—for some it would likely have been the closest we'd come to a sexual encounter in a long time.

A number of us had to receive additional vaccinations required for travel to Iraq. The worst of which, for me at least, was the tetanus vaccine. My entire upper arm and shoulder hurt for two weeks afterwards. Fortunately, most of my vaccinations were up to date, since I had been to Iraq before and had received a full round of shots at that time. Others of our group were not so lucky and had to get a full range of shots for the trip. They walked around for days afterwards with their arms hanging limp by their sides and grim looks on their faces.

Once everything was completed, we left Fort Belvoir and returned to the hotel for the remainder of the day, to make final preparations and pack for our flights—we had been advised that our departures would be staggered over a couple of days. That afternoon, I worked on packing my bags and decided that I needed to mail some items home. At the same time, I reflected, as I knew many others were doing, on what we were all about to embark upon.

I had been notified that I would be flying out of Dulles Airport the next day, along with Stan and Ruby, the husband-and-wife team from Georgia. Our final night in the United States was much like the previous evenings, though mixed with a little restlessness and, perhaps, just a touch of apprehension on all our parts.

My memory is pretty vague about that final night, so it's quite possible that I ended up in Jimmy's room once again. If it was like the previous evenings we spent together, that would account for my loss of memory, but my sleep was definitely restless.

CHAPTER 3

Baghdad or Bust

My Lufthansa flight to Kuwait departed from Dulles Airport in the afternoon and would be a direct flight to Frankfurt, Germany, where there would be a few hours' layover until the departure for Kuwait City. I rode to the airport with Stan and Ruby, but once there we separated until our departure time. I wouldn't really see either of them again until our arrival in Kuwait. I carried a backpack with me onto the plane and stowed it easily into an overhead compartment.

Not much can be said about the flight to Frankfurt, except that it was long and boring. Fortunately, I didn't get seated next to anyone 'difficult'… meaning someone rather large in stature who takes up half of my seat along with their own, or someone whose idea of personal hygiene is far different from mine. I tried to sleep for most of the flight, but I've always had difficulty sleeping on an aircraft. In a previous life I had made this flight across the ocean a couple of dozen times and never was able to get much sleep. Plus, in economy/coach, the seats aren't made for sleeping anyway.

After about eight hours in the air we arrived in Frankfurt. It had been a number of years since I'd last set foot in the Frankfurt *Flughafer*, and it hadn't changed much in that time. I was reminded of something funny that had happened many years earlier, while I was in Germany serving in the army. My parents, who at the time were both in their sixties, had decided to fly to Germany for a visit. Being a member of the military, I was able to get them a discounted flight which made their trip possible. They too had arrived in the Frankfurt Airport and I had driven up from my base in southern Germany to meet them. Like most airports, the one in Frankfurt has a number of shops and restaurants inside the terminal. After I met them, once they had gotten off their plane, we strolled casually through the terminal to get to where my car was parked. My mother looked into the various store windows and gift shops as we walked casually towards the car park, chatting, getting reacquainted and catching up on all the family news and gossip. One shop, which was probably unique to Germany and not one you were going to find in any U.S. airport, was a 'sex shop'. It was a fairly small shop compared to many of the others we passed along the way through the terminal, and its doorway was covered with some hanging, beaded curtains. It was clearly identifiable as an 'adult' store by the semi-explicit merchandise on display in its windows. Apparently, my mother wasn't really paying close attention and I guess the hanging beads in the doorway kind of caught her attention, so she walked right inside. I quickly pointed out to my father what was happening, and within seconds the hanging beads exploded outward in every direction, quickly followed by my mother, who was all flustered and red-faced. It was certainly not something an elderly lady from the Midwest was used to seeing in an airport.

My dad and I had a big chuckle over that and the story was told and retold over the years at every family gathering. I grew up in a family that never passed up an opportunity to publicly embarrass and humiliate each other, though never maliciously and always in a good-natured way. You took it like a man because you knew that you might be on the receiving end this time, but the next time you'd be the one using the skewer on your sibling or parent. My family liked to laugh and poke fun at and with each other, but it was always done in fun.

My thoughts returned to the present as I made my way through the terminal to the gate where I would catch the next leg of my journey to Kuwait City. I don't recall running into Stan and Ruby while waiting, nor do I remember seeing them on the flight to Kuwait, but I'm sure they would have been on the same flight as me. I relaxed at the gate area and didn't wander off, as I didn't want to take a chance of missing my flight. Eventually, the time came to board for the next leg of this marathon trip.

While boarding the aircraft I discovered that the backpack I was carrying would not fit into the overhead compartment on this particular aircraft, as it had on my previous flight. Apparently this was a smaller aircraft than the one we had crossed the ocean in. Nor would the backpack fit under my assigned seat when I tried to stow it there. I approached an attractive, young German flight attendant and tried to explain to her that I was having difficulty stowing my backpack, asking her "What do I do with this, it won't fit under my seat or in the overhead compartment?" I have never had so much difficulty communicating something so simple in my life. She spoke perfect English, but I would've sworn that she didn't understand a word I was saying, that it was all Greek to her. I kept trying to tell her about my backpack not fitting anywhere, and asking what to do, and she kept telling me that I would have to stow it somewhere.

This went back and forth for a couple of minutes, me telling her it wouldn't fit and her telling me to stow it somewhere. I was about ready to tell her to bend over and I'd stow it alright when a slightly older and more senior flight attendant apparently saw that I was starting to get frustrated and approached us. I explained to her that I wasn't trying to be a pain in the ass, I was merely seeking some guidance on what to do with my backpack. The senior flight attendant led me to the front of the aircraft where she took my backpack, tagged it and told me it would be placed in the cargo hold of the aircraft and that I could claim it in Kuwait City. Something told me (later confirmed) that my backpack would not arrive with me in Kuwait, but I returned to my seat, relieved that I had finally got the problem solved. And I kept my distance from the younger flight attendant for the remainder of the flight.

After another five- or six-hour flight, we arrived. The airport in Kuwait City is a modern, cosmopolitan facility, much like you would see anywhere in the Western world. Numerous stores and shops lined the terminal, some of which were surprising for a Muslim country, I thought. There was a Harley Davidson store, a Hard Rock Café, a Starbucks, and countless jewelry stands and shops, where the gold and silver glittered brightly in the windows and display cases.

At the baggage claim area I discovered that I was missing not only my backpack, but also the luggage cart that I had purchased in Virginia to help me carry everything I had brought with me once I got to Baghdad. I was more concerned about the backpack, as it contained my contact lens solution and some other toiletries. I was directed to a nearby office where a Kuwaiti airport official took my information and advised me to check the next day to see if my backpack or cart had showed up.

After clearing Kuwaiti immigration, I proceeded to an office run by KBR (Kellogg, Brown, and Root, the major Halliburton subsidiary providing much of the support to the military and civilians serving in Iraq), to get further instructions and to rest or stretch my legs, whichever was needed. The KBR office had been set aside for contractors arriving in Kuwait City *en route* to Iraq, so it saw a steady influx of passengers transiting through.

The room was kept dark to accommodate those travelers who were trying to catch up on some lost sleep. There were lounge chairs to relax in, coffee and water, and a TV to watch. A representative who was there briefed us on what was to follow. Stan and Ruby also showed up at the office after I did, and after a brief stay we were escorted onto a bus for a ride to the Hilton Hotel. Located right on the Arabian Gulf, we would be staying there for a few days before heading onward into Iraq.

The U.S. government had contracted with the hotel to use it as a transit point for some of the people going to and coming from Iraq, including ICITAP personnel. KBR handled the billeting and processing upon your arrival. We were to stay at the hotel, attend a few briefings and get some additional medical work, and then we would be manifested onto a military flight headed to Baghdad. Once we had been given a flight date, we would travel by bus to a military airfield in order to catch our flight. The exact dates and times were never publicized for security reasons, so we wouldn't know exactly when we would be departing. We were only told that we'd be in Kuwait for two or three days.

We actually stayed in small, two-story villas separated from the main hotel. The villas had large living rooms with televisions, high-speed internet hookups, and comfortable furniture. Actually they were very nice villas, comparable to any four-star hotel in America, and they were located right on the beach looking out onto the Arabian Gulf.

After checking my e-mail to let family know I had made it this far, I decided to take a walk around and get familiar with where I would be staying for at least the next couple of days. The hotel was a rather large and modern facility. As well as the villas, where I was billeted, there was a separate, more traditional hotel section, which was spread along the beach. The entire area was surrounded by fencing and landscaped walls, with security-controlled entry and exit points.

I had brought my camera with me and while I was walking around and taking some snapshots of the hotel and the beach area, I noticed a hotel security guard quickly approaching. "No photo, no photo!" he yelled, sternly. When he got to me he began waving his arms, telling me in broken English that no photos were allowed. I never did understand why we couldn't take photos, but by that time I'd gotten as many as I wanted so I put the camera away, thanked the guard, and walked off.

I mentioned it to the KBR representative and he seemed surprised about it. He didn't know of any official prohibition against photography. I can only assume it had something to do with security concerns about the property's layout becoming known, or something along those lines. In the Middle East, they are very concerned about the potential for terrorism, even though many of them are actively involved in or supportive of terrorists themselves. Go figure.

We had our meals in the hotel's main restaurant, which was very nice—a modern hotel restaurant with a buffet line as well as an *a la carte* menu. Walking to the restaurant, you would pass a number of nice shops and stores, where jewelry could be purchased along with many other items. There was also a barber shop and ladies' salon.

As I strolled casually through the hotel towards the restaurant, I saw a bookstore and decided to wander inside. It had books printed in both Arabic and English and I noticed a large, coffee table-type book about the history of Kuwait, which contained many photos of the modern country. I started browsing through it, and as I turned the pages I got to a section on Saddam Hussein's invasion back in the early 1990s, which resulted in the First Gulf War. While browsing the several pages and photographs devoted to this moment in history, I came to realize that the old adage that 'history is written by the victor' is definitely true, but in this case it was not so much the victor, but instead the benefactor of the victor. According to this book, the Kuwaiti military had defeated Saddam's Iraqi forces and driven them from Kuwait almost single-handedly. There was a single paragraph dedicated to the 'logistical support' provided by the United States. It was amazing—my memory of what actually occurred after Saddam invaded Kuwait is just a little bit different.

With barely concealed disgust I set the book back down and walked away. To this day I regret not buying it, so that I could show it to people and make them understand what really happened during Operation *Desert Shield* under President George H. W. Bush. Apparently, at least according to the Kuwaitis' version, we have been misled all these years by our government. The First Gulf War was a major Kuwaiti victory, one in which we were hardly involved.

The briefings we received from KBR were largely forgettable, as had been all the ones we'd attended up to this point. They covered some of the things we would experience right away upon landing in Baghdad, so that we didn't stumble around like dumbstruck kids. They drew blood from us and offered us Anthrax shots, which we could decline (and which I did). The last thing I wanted right now was an adverse reaction to the Anthrax vaccine. I wasn't really worried about Anthrax being a threat any more in Iraq anyway. After all, hadn't Saddam assured us that he'd gotten rid of all his chemical weapons?

After two relaxing days at the Hilton, Stan, Ruby, and I were informed that we were leaving and would be followed by the rest of our group separately. The next day we again packed our gear and luggage and loaded onto a bus to be taken to the American air base about an hour away to catch our flight to Baghdad. My missing backpack had shown up the day after I arrived in Kuwait and was transported to the hotel for me, but my luggage cart never did show up. Someone somewhere must have seen it and thought they needed it more than I did, so it looked like I was going to be lugging all my gear without the benefit of my very helpful little cart.

Once at the air base, we got off the bus and were told that it would be a few hours before we could board the aircraft and depart for Baghdad. Our luggage was placed into rows on the ground near the bus, to be checked for explosives by sniffer dogs. Once that was completed, the baggage would be 'palletized' by military load-masters and prepared for loading onto the aircraft. We would be flying in a C-130, the workhorse of the air force's transportation command into Baghdad. This would be my first experience in a C-130, and though I knew it wouldn't be first-class seating, I still found it all really interesting and I was kind of excited about it.

Until our departure, I wandered around the area where we had been dropped off and noticed a small Kuwaiti military museum, so I walked inside to check it out. The displays were mainly military equipment and small vehicles, but it was interesting and it killed some time. There were also a couple of fast food outlets nearby.

When our departure time arrived, late in the afternoon, we were told to put on our body armor and Kevlar helmets and prepare to board the aircraft. We were directed towards the flight line, where an aircraft was waiting, its propellers revved up and turning. Once we were given permission to board the aircraft, we lined up single-file and walked up the ramp at the rear, following the direction of the military flight crews. We were told to walk to the front of the aircraft's loading bay and take a seat. I was at the front of the line, so I got an end-of-the-row seat, which gave me a little bit more room than others who were stuck in the middle. There was a row of nylon canvas seats on each side of the aircraft, and two rows of seats back-to-back down the middle of the loading bay. Needless to say, the quarters were very tight indeed. Definitely not first class and not built for comfort.

After we filed onto the plane and took our seats, we were knee-cap touching knee-cap to the people across from us. Once we got strapped in, we sat and waited for the palettes with our baggage to be loaded, by forklift, into the rear hold area of the plane. I found all of this fascinating and watched as the military pros did their work. They had it down to a science and knew exactly where to place things and how to strap them down. The load had to be correctly balanced inside the cargo hold of the aircraft, and the flight crews took pains to make sure everything was done properly. They were true professionals and it was fun to watch them at work.

Finally, the aircraft was loaded and everything (and everybody) strapped in. The rear loading ramp rose up and locked into place, closing off our view to the outside world. I, as surely as everyone else on board the aircraft, sat and wondered what would be waiting for us when we hit the ground again. The flight to Baghdad from Kuwait took about an hour and a half. There was little conversation between passengers and most people just sat quietly, lost in their own thoughts. The noise of the aircraft's engines made it difficult to talk anyway—you had to shout to be heard by anyone. The steady drone of the engines was almost soothing to me and I very nearly fell asleep during the flight.

There were no windows in the bulkhead from which we could look out, but you could tell when we were making our final approach into Baghdad. The aircraft banked steeply and the engines took on a different sound. We came in low and fast for a fairly hard touchdown onto the runway at what had once been Saddam International Airport, but was now Baghdad International Airport, or as everyone referred to it, BIAP (BY-OP). As we taxied to a stop I think everyone was curious what we would see when the loading ramp came down. Would armed insurgents be waiting to shoot all of us or take us hostage and lop off our heads?

There was nothing nearly as dramatic, as it turned out—as we sat there and watched the ramp lower, all we could see were the last few rays of sunlight streaking the sky. It was nearly dark as our baggage palette was removed by a forklift. A few minutes later, we were instructed by the flight crew to stand up and exit the aircraft in single file. We followed each other towards the rear of the aircraft and walked down the ramp.

The noise was deafening as we walked out onto the tarmac. We followed a pathway painted onto the pavement, and also the hand signals and instructions given by one of the air force ground crew members guiding our way. With the C-130 propellers still turning and its engines rumbling, nearby helicopter rotors 'whomp-whomp-whomping', and large electric power generators running constantly, it was difficult to hear anything at all. Spoken, or should I say shouted words, were mostly inaudible. Everything had to be guided by hand signals. We were directed over to an area off the tarmac and instructed to wait there until the palette containing our luggage had been off-loaded. Then we could collect our belongings and move on to our next stop, further away from the flight line.

On solid ground finally, after our fairly short and uncomfortable flight, we were able to stretch our legs a bit and take in our surroundings, or at least what we could see in the dark and the haze of dust that seemed to float in the air. There wasn't much to see really, as there was limited lighting due to the wartime conditions. Around us was mostly military equipment—tents, sandbags and other temporary buildings—but you could see and sense a lot of human activity going on. In fact it was a hive of activity. You couldn't help but notice the ever-present HESCO barriers around buildings and tents, and anywhere the military felt a need for additional barriers. If you don't know what a HESCO is, it's a simple invention that probably made someone a huge bundle of money. It comprises four connected sections of hard wire mesh. When stood upright and unfolded, it opens up into four sides of a square-shaped structure (each section is approximately four feet by four feet in size, though they do make them in different sizes). These structures are then wrapped around a cloth or canvas sack that slips down inside. A load of dirt or sand is then dropped inside the sacks, filling the HESCO to the top. They are designed to be used as protective barriers and are pretty effective at stopping most ammunition, as well as debris from explosions. They are also pretty effective at stopping moving vehicles. HESCO 'walls' and barriers are around most U.S. buildings and facilities throughout Iraq. For that matter, they are present in most bases and outposts where there are U.S. troops in isolated or Third World countries. It's a pretty effective and low-cost way of fortifying a base or building and providing a pretty fair level of security.

In the areas where there was lighting you could see lots of activity, with people walking back and forth. Some of them were actually preparing to board the same C-130 that we had just exited, for a return flight to the air base we had just left in Kuwait—contractors and soldiers going home for good, or for an R&R or a reassignment. I'm sure they were all happy to be getting out of Baghdad in one piece, and with all their pieces.

Once our baggage reached the staging area at the side of the tarmac, we were allowed to reclaim our gear and proceed over to where a bus was parked for a short drive to Camp Stryker and what was affectionately referred to as 'the Stables'. The Stables are sandbag- and HESCO-surrounded tents, with cots erected for the use of soldiers and civilians transiting BIAP *en route* to other areas of Iraq, or awaiting manifest on a flight back home. At the billeting office we were issued a set of sheets and a pillow and given a tent assignment. We also checked in with someone who took our names and put us on the list for a flight into the Green Zone. The tents held about 40 people on military cots and weren't built for comfort or long-term residents. It was merely a place where you could lay down and stretch out and try to grab some shut-eye before moving on to wherever you were headed next. By the time you got there you were usually so tired that the accommodation didn't matter too much.

Male and female alike, everyone was thrown into the same tent regardless of gender. There was certainly no privacy there. Stan and Ruby ended up on cots in the same tent as I did. Unfortunately for them, their choice of the only two unoccupied cots that were side-by-side just happened to be right next to the world's snoring champion. The next morning they both complained about how they'd got little if any sleep during the night. Thankfully, I found a cot in a far corner away from any snorers and was able to actually get some sleep. Considering how tired I was by this time though, I doubt that even the world's snoring champion would have kept me awake.

The next morning I ventured out, trying to get some bearings on my new temporary lodgings with the benefit of daylight. Camp Stryker had a small PX, an MWR tent (Morale, Welfare and Recreation, which had internet and phone services so you could contact loved ones back home, letting them know you had made it to Baghdad and were alright), and a chow hall for meals. Plus lots and lots of 'Porta-Potties'. The chow hall was excellent—you could never complain about the food over there. The old saying 'an army travels on its stomach' was definitely adhered to at the major bases in Iraq.

The ground was covered for the most part with what you might call round river stones—smooth with no sharp edges. You'd think they'd be easy to walk on but that wasn't necessarily the case. The ground was covered a few inches deep with these stones and it actually made walking difficult. They would slide beneath your feet so that actually moving forward was much more difficult than it was on pavement.

At the Stables billeting office we were also instructed that we would have to go back out to the flight line the next day, to try to get manifested for Blackhawk helicopter transportation into Baghdad. At the time we arrived in Iraq, the BIAP highway to the Green Zone had been closed for vehicular travel due to constant attacks by the insurgency. Sometimes multiple attacks took place in a 24-hour period. Route Irish, as it was called, was considered the most dangerous stretch of road in the world at the time of our arrival. Ground transport from BIAP to the Green Zone had therefore been suspended except for military patrols, so a steady stream of Blackhawk helicopters played taxi cab for everyone going into, or coming out of, the Green Zone. The cost of fuel and maintenance on the 'birds' had to be enormous. Since helicopters were being used the payload was limited—one bird carried passengers while an accompanying chopper carried baggage.

After breakfast the next morning, we proceeded out to the flight line with all of our gear to try to get manifested and await transportation into Baghdad. Unfortunately, neither Stan and Ruby nor I were able to get a flight out that day and we had to stay another night in the Stables—another very unpleasant evening listening to people snoring. The next day we made our way to the flight line again, dragging our luggage and gear, once again in the hopes of getting a flight into the Green Zone. While waiting around, you could grab a bite to eat from the cases of MREs (Meals, Ready to Eat) which were stacked everywhere. You just opened a case, grabbed a meal, and checked the stamp on the outside of each individual meal to see what you were getting. Some were actually not too bad—chili con carne was my favorite. They had a chemical heating element inside the packet, which heated the meal up by just adding water.

After a wait of several hours, we were finally advised by someone at the 'trans office' tent that it was going to be our turn to load onto a chopper for the flight into Baghdad, with our baggage on a second chopper. Blackhawk flights always travel in pairs, in case one aircraft goes down or develops mechanical trouble. We put on our body armor and Kevlar helmets and loaded onto the helicopter. A Blackhawk holds about eight passengers and I was fortunate in landing a window seat. Actually there was no window, just a large opening to look out of. As with the C-130, this would be my first flight on a Blackhawk. I found this prospect exciting as well, but tried to hide my emotions so as not to appear like a 'new guy'. In Iraq you have to look cool, by wearing cargo pants, tactical vests, sunglasses, and weapons of every sort hanging off your body, and you can't display any fear or intimidation at any time. And no one ever admits to just arriving in country.

Our flight to Baghdad was uneventful and, as far as I was concerned, over far too quickly. I enjoyed seeing the Iraqi countryside and parts of the city from above during the flight. Flying over the city, you were separated from the car bombings and small-arms fire that was part of the daily life for Iraqis and coalition forces as well. As we cruised at several hundred feet, the ground seemed to move so fast beneath the chopper, as I looked out of the open side, that it was almost dizzying.

I recognized the moment when we passed into the Green Zone, as I could see the Crossed Swords boulevard and other buildings and structures, and the high concrete blast walls I had seen all over Iraq before. Shortly after this, we began our descent into a large parking lot area, not far from Saddam's former main palace in the heart of Baghdad, which was serving as the coalition forces headquarters and the U.S. Embassy.

CHAPTER 4

Never Have So Many Done So Little for So Much

When we landed in the Green Zone, we were met by a man named Barney, a representative from the ICITAP/CPATT program (International Criminal Investigation Training Assistance Program/Civilian Police Assistance Training Team. It seems that ICITAP wasn't a big enough acronym, they needed to add to it). Barney was a decent enough guy, but having dealt with so many new people coming in and asking him the same questions he had answered countless times before, his patience level wasn't what it once had been. "Toss them in the back," Barney said as we loaded our gear into the back of a pickup truck and then climbed inside the cab. We then drove a short distance towards our new temporary home, the Adnan Palace, where much of the police program was located and run from, and where we would be billeted in a large tent for more than two weeks, drawing full pay while sitting around and doing nothing. Later the next day we would be officially welcomed into the CPATT family in Iraq.

The Adnan Palace was a large, somewhat pyramid-shaped structure, which had at one time been a residence for one of Saddam Hussein's daughters and her husband. Garish and tasteless both inside and out, much like all of Saddam's own palaces. There was a large swimming pool behind it, which was devoid of water. If you weren't paying attention at night, you could walk right into the deep end of an empty swimming pool, since there really wasn't anything in place to prevent an accidental tumble—no barricades, lights, or warning signs.

We arrived at the palace and had to make it through the checkpoint security to get access into the compound. The vehicle was searched inside and out, the guards using mirrors on long sticks to check the vehicle's undercarriage. Most of the checkpoint guards were private contractors hired from Iraq. Considering the unemployment level in Iraq at the time, and the ongoing reconstruction efforts, finding jobs for Iraqis was an important part of the equation. The guards looked like they were just going through the motions but seemed efficient enough.

There were so many companies trying to cash in on the billions floating around Iraq, with many of them hiring guards from other Third World countries to keep costs low and profits high. There were Nepalese, Ugandans, South Americans, even Fijians. Companies went wherever they could obtain cheap labor. Supposedly all had prior military experience from their home countries, but I sincerely doubt those from Uganda or Fiji were of quite the same caliber as the American forces.

Later, we would discover that our perimeter security guards at the Baghdad Police Academy were indeed from Fiji—very friendly individuals, always smiling and waving at us as we walked around the inside of the compound. The only problem with that was that the bad guys would be coming from outside the compound, which is where their attention should have been directed. On more than one occasion I would yell up to one of them to keep a watch on the other direction. They readily complied, smiling while they did so, but soon thereafter you'd see them waving again at someone else walking inside the compound. There was little sense of comfort from having their eagle eyes on the job and, once I received it, I drew my M-4 carbine a little closer to my bunk at night when I slept, and made sure I kept a weapon with me at all times during the day.

After we passed through the checkpoint at the Adnan Palace entrance, we drove a short distance to a small parking area near a large tent surrounded by sandbags. We got out of the vehicle with all our gear and Barney led us into the sandy-colored tent, which was about 40 feet long by 25 feet wide, with an entrance on both ends. Inside the tent, running down the middle, there were about 20 sets of bunk beds, separated by wall lockers—the wall lockers being that in name only, since they mostly didn't lock or even allow the doors to close securely. Some were even without doors entirely.

The bunkbeds were placed end-to-end up against each other, running the length of the tent. Near one end of the tent were a few hard, white, plastic lawn furniture-type tables and chairs, a large-screen TV, and a refrigerator with a supply of bottled water. Magazines and other reading material lay strewn across the tables. Spaced along the tent walls were combination heater/air-conditioning units, three on each side of the tent. Since ICITAP had received advanced notice of Stan and Ruby's arrival, a small section in one corner of the tent had been blocked off with wall lockers, making a sort of bedroom for them, giving the married couple a little privacy away from the rest of us. It was ICITAP/CPATT's version of a honeymoon suite.

The Adnan Palace compound was fairly large and consisted of row upon row of the same large tents that we were staying in, each with sandbag walls built up along the sides and the ends of each tent. There were perhaps six or eight tents in all. They all looked exactly alike, and if you weren't paying attention you could walk right past the tent you lived in and go inside the wrong one. There were also a few concrete bunkers placed here and there, where you could hunker down during a mortar attack. The bunkers were shaped like an upside down letter 'U', about 12- or 15-feet long and open on each end. Maybe eight or so people could huddle together inside in case mortar rounds started raining in on the compound.

The first floor of the Adnan Palace had been turned into office spaces around a large circular atrium. The upper floors were being used by Iraqi and U.S. military officials. CPATT also had an office with internet service, and a training room in a small theater located off the main foyer. The atrium was pretty much the same as all the other palaces and buildings associated with the Saddam Hussein regime—all were gaudy and ostentatious. On the palace grounds were the tents that were being used as classrooms for some of the higher-ranking Iraqi police, as well as newly arriving police trainers such as ourselves. There was also a chow hall tent, again surrounded by sandbags, which the Iraqi students and some Americans used. In addition there was a small restaurant in an adjoining building, which was affectionately named 'the Baghdad Country Club', but we took most of our meals at a military chow hall that was a short ride on the bus.

The compound, like most others in Iraq, was surrounded by high concrete walls, with several elevated guard towers along the perimeter staffed by armed contract security forces. Once again, you had to be cleared through an armed checkpoint to gain access to the Adnan compound, and in order to be admitted you better have your CAC card clearly displayed. Most of us had purchased lanyards to hang our cards around our necks, or small ID cases that could fit around your arm with elastic straps. The mandatory display of CAC cards was required on any military installation.

If you carried a weapon, you had to ensure it was unloaded by clearing (unloading) it at a clearing barrel set up at the checkpoint. No rounds in the chamber were allowed. Even though, as police officers, none of us had ever carried an unloaded weapon, we were guests of the military so we followed their rules... for the most part, as far as they knew anyway, with the exception of General Order No. 1 (the prohibition against alcohol).

Picture an average small-college football stadium back in America, and that would be about the size comparison of the Adnan Palace compound, obviously minus the high walls of a football stadium. It included the palace structure itself, the empty Olympic-size swimming pool, and some other smaller outbuildings. It was surrounded completely by high concrete 'T-walls'. T-walls, blast walls, they were one and the same, and they were all over Iraq. They served as the exterior perimeter walls for all U.S. bases, the entire Green Zone, and other public buildings and compounds throughout the country. They were made of reinforced concrete and looked like an upside-down letter 'T'. They were roughly two-feet thick, with the base thicker, and most were around 20 feet tall, some even topped with barbed wire. T-walls also surrounded many of the buildings inside a fortified compound for added protection.

The Adnan Palace was also near the military parade boulevard built by Saddam for official celebrations and parades. It had a large reviewing stand about midway down the boulevard, and at each end of the boulevard were the large Crossed Swords statues. The hands and forearms holding the swords were supposedly sculpted from Saddam's own hands. They formed an arch across the boulevard and met in the middle about sixty or eighty feet above the surface of the road. Next to this was the Tomb of the Unknown Soldier memorial. The Baghdad Zoo, or what was left of it was also nearby. There was also a memorial park with a few ancient fighter jet airplanes that had been on display at one point in time. The Tomb of the Unknown Soldier was located off one end of the parade boulevard, standing alone. It looked basically like a large dinner plate, maybe 80 feet or more across and resting atop a 40-foot tall pedestal, with the red, black, and green of the Iraqi flag added in. It was a rather gaudy and ostentatious display, as was typical with Saddam's palaces and everything else that he constructed. 'Tacky' was the watchword that Iraqi architects adhered to, it would seem.

The ground cover in this area reminded me of the desert in the southwest of the U.S., with only a little vegetation, mostly scrub brush mixed in with a few small trees—no grass anywhere, but dust and sand everywhere. Perhaps at one time it had been well maintained, with manicured lawns and shrubs, but after all the years of United Nations sanctions, not to mention war, the entire area had fallen into a state of serious disrepair.

The weather in Baghdad this time of year was fairly mild. It was hot enough to need air conditioning during the day time, but at night the temperatures dipped down to the low 40s and even upper 30s, making it just chilly enough that those of us who are 'cold blooded' needed some heat turned on inside the tent overnight. This turned into a point of irritation between the warm-blooded and cold-blooded people of our group, with each of us sneaking over to the units when no one was looking and adjusting the temperature—only to have someone else sneak over when you weren't looking and change it back.

Once we were billeted in the tent, Barney turned us over to a guy named 'Lenny', who as best we could tell was sort of in charge of logistics for the Adnan Palace. Toothless, and about 50–55 years old with a scruff of a beard on his chin, he immediately commenced to regale us with stories of his derring-do as a police officer, as well as during his service in Iraq. He instructed us on how to properly carry our M-4 carbines (which had not been waiting for us on our arrival, contrary to what we had been promised) in order to be able to rapidly engage the enemy when involved in gunplay on the streets of Baghdad. Lenny's 'heroics' might have made you look at him in awe as a 'super cop' if you didn't know any better. Those of us who knew better quietly rolled our eyes as we looked at each other and mouthed 'bullshit artist' when Lenny wasn't looking.

Lenny claimed that he had been the chief of police for a community in the Midwest of the United States. His resume might have sounded impressive to the uninformed, but since one of my daughters had attended college nearby I was quite familiar with the community where he worked—a small spot on the map which was basically nothing more than a radar trap along a roadway. It was not the thriving, challenging metropolis that he tried to portray it as, and certainly not one to produce the gun battles and acts of derring-do Lenny claimed to have participated in. Though I don't know the exact numbers for certain, the police department he worked for was very small, likely no more than a 'chief' and one or two other officers, and probably part time officers at that. In many very small communities like this anywhere in the States, the police chief is usually related to the mayor or other important people in the town, and not necessarily hired for their professionalism, education, or skills.

While giving us a tour of the compound, Lenny took us over to a small building which sat next to a large metal gate, which looked more like a metal wall. As we were told by Lenny, right on the other side of the gate was the so-called 'Red Zone', where the bad guys were. There was nothing preventing them from driving a car or truck right up to or even through the gate and blowing themselves up, or jumping out of the vehicle and firing their AK-47s at anything that moved inside the Adnan Palace compound. It was not a very comforting thought at that particular moment in our tour of the palace grounds, but we later found out that Lenny's description of the bad guys' proximity to us was wildly exaggerated, as was everything else that he told us.

Lenny kept an office and a bunk inside this small building by the metal gate. Inside, he pointed out his collection of DVDs, which covered an entire wall. Lenny told us we could watch as many as we wanted.

We never asked him how many of them were porno, but I suspect that there was an exhaustive supply.

Lenny also prided himself on being able to obtain just about anything you might need, though his means of obtaining things was left to conjecture. I never quite knew which side of the law Lenny was on—a typical 'scrounger' of the first order, it would seem. He was definitely a self-promoter and very likely his scrounging efforts were exaggerated as well. We didn't really care too much as we didn't figure on having that much contact with him. Our stay at this location was expected to be short. Little did we know it would last quite a while, at least three weeks.

The Green Zone was an approximately four-square-mile, highly fortified area in the heart of Baghdad, on the west side of the Tigris River. It was a fairly secured area, where the American and other foreign embassies were located, along with the Multi-National Force headquarters. The main hospital, the 28th Combat Support Hospital (called the 'CASH'), was also located there. The court facilities where Saddam Hussein would eventually be put on trial was also located within the confines of the fortified walls surrounding the Green Zone. Many government-contracting offices and private-contracting companies were located there as well. An effort had been underway by the powers-that-be to get people to start calling the Green Zone by a different name, calling it the 'International Zone' or 'IZ' instead. Most likely some diplomat came up with that, thinking it didn't sound as ominous as 'the Green Zone'. By this time the U.S. government and the military were already trying to change the image of our effort in Iraq.

As I mentioned earlier, the Adnan Palace itself once belonged to Saddam's daughter (now a widow) and her husband. Unfortunately for Saddam's daughter, her husband had reportedly defected to Jordan a number of years earlier. As the story goes, he was later enticed into returning to Baghdad and told that Saddam was letting bygones be bygones. When he arrived, he was rushed off to a waiting helicopter and unceremoniously thrown out from a few thousand feet up in the air. Hence Saddam's daughter being a widow. I can't attest to the accuracy of this account but it makes for a good story, and that's the story we were told. Suffice to say that Saddam's son-in-law is taking a dirt nap somewhere in Iraq, whether for parachuting out of a helicopter without a parachute or through some other cause, and Saddam's daughter was indeed a widow.

Even though the Green Zone was mostly secure, we were advised by those who had arrived before us that we shouldn't leave the compound without an armed escort, as we had not yet been issued our M-4 carbines or Beretta 9mm pistols. We had been told back in Virginia that as soon as we hit the ground in Baghdad we would be issued weapons, but that just wasn't the case. It was just the first of many things we were told that we would find out weren't true.

The PX and a military chow hall were a short drive away from the Adnan Palace, and we could check out a full-sized armored SUV to drive there if we chose to. Again, without weapons we weren't really comfortable and didn't want to travel too far from our compound. There was a shuttle bus operating within the confines of the Green Zone. It would pick you up at designated bus stops—one being the Adnan Palace—and then transport you to the CASH hospital, to Saddam's palace (which housed the embassy and military headquarters), the PX, and some other locations within the zone. We were told it was safe but to me it looked like a nice, large, slow-moving target for an insurgency RPG. The only thing the buses were lacking was a red and white target circle painted on the sides, the back, and the roof.

Two experienced police trainers, Don and another man whose name I've forgotten, were inside our tent when we arrived and gave us the lowdown on what to expect, as well as other useful information, such as where in the zone you could purchase a six-pack of beer. This was the first time we heard of Café Napoli, located on a section of Route Irish just before it led out of the Green Zone and into 'injun territory'. Route Irish was the main road to and from BIAP and the Green Zone, which, as I previously mentioned, had been closed to all vehicular travel by contractors because of the constant attacks.

After getting settled into our tent, I walked over to the palace building to see if I could send some emails back home, letting loved ones know that I had arrived safely. That was pretty much the routine for the next couple of days, until the arrival of the remainder of our group from

Lorton, Virginia. The internet room was located off the main atrium of the palace. It was a room about 20 feet in length by around 15 feet wide, and there was a large conference table in the middle, surrounded by chairs. The table top was covered with Ethernet cables for hooking up laptops. Accessing the internet presented a challenge, since there were only six Ethernet cables and it seemed like there was always a dozen people trying to hook up.

Once settled into the tent at the Adnan Palace, we all established our daily routine, which involved eating breakfast taking the bus to the PX, eating lunch at a nearby military chow hall, checking email, going back to the PX to stare at the shelves and counters for anything new that may have shown up, eating dinner, showering, watching DVDs, sitting around and bullshitting, and then going to bed. Not necessarily in that order. There was simply little else we could do.

"You guys thirsty?" Don asked one day. He had already been accommodating enough to take us on a few beer runs to Café Napoli. Being a beer drinker (in moderation) I would always opt for a case of Corona, which could usually be found at Café Napoli, but you took whatever they had—beggars can't be choosers. At different times, Café Napoli had Corona, Heineken, Amstel, and others, including a very dusty case of Budweiser on one occasion. You just never knew what they would have in stock at the time that you visited. They usually had a steady supply of hard liquor and wines too, since they took up less room than cases of beer in their small supply closet. Alcohol was a way to soothe the pain of tent-living and relax a little, and no one in our group ever got out of line with it. There's nothing wrong with relaxing with a drink or two in the evening after a long day of… relaxing and doing nothing.

We jokingly called the trips to Café Napoli 'tactical beer runs', because they took on some elements of a military operation. When we arrived, one person would stay outside with the vehicle to make sure nobody tampered with it, while the other two entered the restaurant. Once inside, one person would haggle with the proprietor while the other stood armed watch over any Iraqis that happened to be inside.

Café Napoli was situated in the middle of some high-rise apartment buildings. It was a rather nondescript building from the outside, and if not for the sign identifying it in English, no one would really know that it was a restaurant and, more importantly, a liquor store in the heart of Baghdad.

As we arrived and parked our SUV outside the café, there were no other vehicles parked anywhere nearby. I went inside with Don while a guy named Bill, who had accompanied us on this trip, stayed outside with our vehicle. Don and I entered the café and my radar immediately went up, as there were several Iraqis seated inside at tables, having coffee or a bite to eat.

We walked up to the unsmiling Iraqi proprietor behind a small counter and he asked in good English, "How can I help you?" Don kept a wary eye on the diners as I asked the proprietor if I could get a case of beer. He nodded, stepped away from the counter, walked over to a doorway and opened the door. From what I could see inside there were cases of beer stacked atop each other, as well as bottles of alcohol and wine. I saw a case of Corona right on top and said "I'll take the Corona. How much do I owe you?" The proprietor said "Thirty dollars." I reached into my pocket, pulled out a wad of cash, peeled off $30 and handed it to the man, who simply nodded and took the money. I grabbed the case of Corona that he had set onto the counter and Don and I walked out. Never once did the man break a smile or really make much eye contact. Some of the Iraqis sitting inside had looked on passively while our haggling took place, some with a bemused look on their face, others with barely hidden hostility. It was not your typical shopping trip to the local liquor store back in the United States.

Many Iraqis still lived inside the Green Zone, in high-rise buildings and single standing structures. They hadn't been displaced simply because the U.S. and coalition forces had selected their part of the city for the embassies and military headquarters, but you had no way of knowing where their loyalties might lie. There had, in fact, been isolated attacks against Westerners inside the Green Zone, and some people had even been killed. A year or so earlier, an American who had been working out at a gym had been walking home after dark when he was stabbed and killed. As far as I know, his murder was never solved.

We loaded into our SUV and headed back to the Adnan Palace. As we arrived, we had to go through the checkpoint again and then we drove over to our tent and unloaded. I took my case of Corona inside and put it in the large refrigerator—a nice cold beer was going to taste good later that evening. There was a lot of sharing among our group, no one ever really kept track of who drank what. We figured it would all even out in the end.

The routine at the Adnan Palace didn't vary greatly from day to day for the first week of our stay, and intense boredom began to set in. You can't take cops who are Type A personalities, used to 'doing something', and shove them into a tent with little or no distractions without them becoming antsy.

When we arrived there was no such thing as an orientation program in place, but the management, in their wisdom, eventually determined something needed and put a program together. Like much of what we had experienced so far, it was less than memorable, but at least they had made the effort, and they deserve credit for that. There really should have been a regular and more formal new-arrival orientation, one that addressed all the questions someone might have when landing in a war zone. Instead, we got a steady stream of 'window or aisle' responses, and few questions were ever answered. There was simply no interest about what anyone outside the Green Zone clique had to say.

Though we did have a television inside the tent, you can only watch so many DVDs before that too begins to grate on your nerves. There are always differing tastes on what programming to watch as well. The internet café inside the palace was always a challenge too. There were too many newly arrived instructors, not to mention the palace cadre who were also vying for computer time. Everyone tried to be courteous and limit their internet use to family emails, but at times it got frustrating, waiting for your turn. Some people would wait until the wee hours of the morning, since there were fewer people up and about at that time of night. The time difference between Baghdad and the U.S. was around 12 hours, so you might even catch your loved ones up and be able to chat using instant messaging. Since it was an unsecure system, you had to keep in mind 'OPSEC' (operational security), and avoid too much detail about your location, surroundings, movements, and what you were doing. It was also a good idea to limit information about your loved ones back home as well. You just never knew who might be listening in.

The best word I can use to describe the rest of the facilities at the compound is 'austere'. We had a Porta-Potty right outside the tent, which was always disgusting to use. The smell alone was usually a good reason not to go in there. It did, however, provide us with one diversion from the boring routine, which was watching some local Iraqi empty it. It wasn't done as it would be back in America, where they have trucks with vacuum pumps that suck out the filth. These Porta-Potties were emptied out by hand.

One of the Iraqi workers would use a hand-held cup, fashioned out of an old bleach bottle, and reach into the bottom tank of the Porta-Potty to scoop out whatever solids were inside. Others used a tin can that had been soldered to a straightened-out wire clothes hanger. We called them 'shit-dippers', and many off-color jokes were made about this being a job they would hand down from father to son, a generational kind of thing. Jokes were also made about 'parents' career day' at school. We would double over in laughter as one of our group would explain, in great detail, how it would play out at an Iraqi elementary school.

"Let me introduce my dad Abdul. My dad is a shit-dipper. He empties out portable toilets for a living. He has brought along some of the tools of his trade to share with you all. This is his 'bleach bottle', which he sometimes uses to reach down into the bottom of the Porta-Potty to scoop out poop. He also uses this metal clothes hanger with this Campbell's soup can soldered onto the end of it. This allows him to reach down deeper when necessary. *Don't touch anything!*"

Needless to say, the jokes were almost endless. After dipping the Porta-Potty out, the Iraqi would then spray it down with chemicals to sanitize it. Though no one ever felt comfortable actually sitting down inside one of them, they did come in handy in the middle of the night when that beer you'd consumed started wanting to come out.

There were regular toilet facilities inside the palace, which most of us used for longer, 'sit-down' visits. The bathrooms in the palace were quite ornate, with gilding on the sinks and commodes and marble everywhere. You almost felt like you were taking a 'royal dump' when using them.

One evening, a night-time visit to the Porta-Potty by one of our group provided us with one of the more memorable moments. Roy woke up in the middle of the night and got out of his bunk in order to pay a visit to the 'PP'. When he returned, as there were no lights on inside the tent, he misjudged which was his bunk and tried to climb into bed with another of our group, a fairly large male named Wallie. Since Wallie was a happily married man and wasn't really interested in sharing his bunk, or being 'spooned' by Roy, he very loudly objected.

"What the hell are you doing?" he shouted, breaking the silence of the night. All of a sudden there was a very loud 'thump', the sound of something large hitting the floor. Kenny, who was in the bunk above Wallie, had laughed so hard at what was happening below him that he'd fallen out of bed and landed directly on his head. Kenny let out a yelp, and needless to say the situation attracted much attention from the rest of us. The story has been told and retold ever since, with many embellishments I'm sure, but I swear my telling is probably the most accurate. I've always wondered, though, how someone loses their balance while lying down in a bed.

There was also a small shower trailer next to the Porta-Potty. It was 'co-ed', so Stan had to remain outside and guard the door while his wife was inside. It certainly wasn't the nicest shower, but it was better than nothing. It consisted of about five stalls, as well as sinks with wall-mounted mirrors for shaving and brushing teeth. The water wasn't safe for drinking, so you had to bring a bottle of water to rinse out your mouth after brushing your teeth. These shower trailers had something of a reputation in Iraq, since some had been improperly installed by cheap labor recruited from Third World countries. KBR cutting costs had resulted in a couple of American soldiers being electrocuted while using such shower trailers at bases in Iraq. I always made sure I took my showers in daylight so I would not have to flip the light switch.

After over a week, we were finally advised that the staff had developed a new presentation, and we would have the privilege of being the first group of new instructors to attend the 'ICITAP Iraq Orientation'. One of the Adnan staff, a guy named Melvin, stopped by the tent one afternoon and asked me to spread the word.

"Have everybody report to the Palace tomorrow at 10," he said. "We have an orientation program finally put together and tomorrow will be day one. We'll fill in the schedule for the rest of the week at that time."

By now we were all looking for something to break the monotony so we welcomed the change in our schedule. Unfortunately we would find out that the orientation wasn't very useful and only took up a couple of hours of the day. Created more to give us something to do other than just lay around, it was certainly not memorable. Little of the content has stuck with me, but one thing I do recall is that some of it would now be considered very politically incorrect. The PowerPoint presentation was interspersed with a few photos of naked women, some funny video clips, and other more ribald and off-color humor—not much different from the police roll calls many of us had attended when we worked back in the States. Oh yeah, and the slogan they opened the briefings with would become more or less the motto of the ICITAP program in Iraq: 'Never have so many done so little for so much'.

I recall one day, sitting in the theater conference room and watching a steady stream of uninformed, unhelpful, pompous asses from the Green Zone ICITAP staff standing before us and trying to fill up time. The briefings were simply not done well, as though they had been thrown together to give us something to do. They answered few of the questions we all had about the Baghdad Academy, or the other places we were headed in the Iraqi Theater of Operations. And 'window or aisle' was repeated regularly if any of us asked a question they didn't want to answer.

On one day, an Iraqi police officer was invited to speak (with the help of a translator) about how the police operated in his country. He appeared quite ill-at-ease in the position he'd been placed in, and though his heart was in the right place, little of substance was gleaned from this exercise. Our interest was in how the police operated, patrolled, and responded to calls for service. What we got was an explanation of the Iraqi police rank structure. The gist was that Iraqi police operations weren't even close to what we had experienced with our own departments back home. Responding to calls for service was basically unheard of. Citizens would have to come to the police station to report a crime or express a grievance. There were no real neighborhood watch or patrols by police in squad cars. It was a very unresponsive service. *This* was what we were supposed to build upon. It was certainly a challenge, and one made even harder because of the early decision by the Bush administration to disband the Iraqi police to rid it of any Baathist Party holdovers.

During a question-and-answer period, my colleagues tried to elicit more practical information from the Iraqi police officer, with little success. He was unresponsive, since our questions were based upon our own experiences and were concepts he just didn't really understand. At the end of his briefing, our understanding of the Iraqi police force was pretty much what it had been before he'd started—minimal.

During a brief break in the presentation, I asked the ICITAP briefer about when we would be receiving weapons, as we had been promised they would be waiting for us when we arrived. He told us that we'd get them soon and if we didn't want to wait, then 'window or aisle'. We continued to be assured that we were safe in the Green Zone and didn't really need weapons anyway—but these assurances came from staff who were walking around with 9mm pistols strapped to their thighs. It was easy for them to say we were safe and didn't need anything.

During one orientation session, while being put to sleep by one of the presenters, Ruby received a visit from an unwelcome guest. As the presentation droned on we suddenly heard a screech of terror from where Ruby was seated. "What the fuck!" she screamed. It seems that a large rat had fallen from the ceiling, about 20 feet above where she was seated, and dropped right into her lap. Needless to say, it got Ruby's attention and then she got ours. The rat scurried away, giving our group our first experience with Iraqi insurgents. In this case it's probably good that we weren't armed because Ruby, and a few others, might have popped off a few rounds at the rat as it ran away.

The days seemed to run into each other as the boredom of our existence wore on all of us. The U.S. government was paying us over $13,000 per month to sit on our behinds in a tent in the Green Zone, watching DVDs, surfing the internet, visiting the PX, eating, and drinking a few beers in the evenings. Finally, after about a week, we were advised by

Melvin that the following day a representative from the large civilian contractor DynCorp would be bringing our weapons. "You all need to be up at the Palace at 11 for weapon issuance," he told us.

The CPATT staff had been telling us that it was generally pretty safe where we were and that we shouldn't make a big deal out of not having weapons yet, but that's not something to tell street cops who had grown accustomed to the feel of a weapon on their hips. We were all used to deciding for ourselves where, when and how we were 'safe'. Had we not been told back in Virginia that we would be issued weapons upon our arrival, it might have been a bit easier to deal with, but we felt that we had been misled and we were all uncomfortable being so close to a war while unarmed. We were all volunteers and knew the dangers when we signed up, but we at least wanted to be able to defend ourselves if 'Haji' came over the wire and into our compound. As it was, about the only thing we could do in an insurgent attack would be to toss rocks or maybe a few empty beer bottles at them. Not much defense against an AK-47 or an RPG.

CHAPTER 5

Just Give Us a Damn Gun

The next day, 'Marty' from DynCorp showed up at the appointed time
and we were all ushered into the same auditorium where we had been
holding our orientation briefings. We met together to sign for the
M-4 carbines and Beretta pistols, and the ammunition that we would
each be issued. Finally, after a couple of weeks in Iraq, we were getting
weapons. I think there was an inaudible sigh of relief among our group.
The process went pretty smoothly and, once completed, Marty left and
we returned to our tent, where we sat down and started loading the
magazines that came with our weapons. We were finally able to strap on
our side-arms and feel more comfortable. At least now we knew we'd
have a fighting chance if the insurgents ever decided to pay us a visit.
Plus it just felt more natural—cops get so used to wearing a weapon
on their side that it becomes second nature and they don't even realize
it. It becomes a part of their body. We all felt whole once again, and
no longer naked.

Once the issuing of weapons was out of the way, our day fell into
pretty much the same pattern we had followed up to that point. Some
of us went to the PX and others just wandered around the Adnan
Palace compound or hung out in the tent. Later that night, despite the
assurances that were in a very safe and secure environment, there was
what appeared to be a large-scale firefight about 300 meters away, near
what would become the courthouse where the Saddam Hussein trial
would take place. Sometime after dark we were roused by the sound
of small-arms fire and explosions coming from east of our compound.

We all scrambled out of the tent and looked at each other with concern. Near to our tent there was a perimeter guard tower, so I climbed up the ramp to get a visual, to try to understand what was happening.

In the darkness it was difficult to see exactly what was taking place, but there was obviously a lot of shooting and flashes of light off in the distance. Stan and Ruby stood down below the guard tower watching and I reported back to them what little I could see of what was taking place. Stan and Ruby looked concerned, and I felt the same way.

"Can you see what's going on?" Ruby asked.

"Not much really," I responded. "Just a lot of light flashes and shooting."

Both Stan and Ruby had faced dangerous situations before, but this was something new. All of us were in a strange environment and facing potential threats we had never faced before, and had only heard about on the evening news back home. I'll admit to a recurring dream I had some nights about getting captured by the insurgents and having my head lopped off by a terrorist like Abu Musab al Zarqawi, who was running around Baghdad at that time. He was doing just that, lopping off captured Westerners' heads. It was not a pleasant night for me when that dream popped into my head, I can assure you.

The distinct sound of automatic small-arms fire, as well as what looked like muzzle flashes, could be clearly seen and heard off in the distance. We watched with rapt attention as the firefight appeared to move around the base of what would become the Iraqi courthouse. Occasionally a small explosion would interrupt the gunfire. It was a very confusing situation for us spectators, and it lasted for approximately 15 minutes, with my colleagues and I having a front-row seat from behind the compound walls.

During the firefight our small group also experienced its first 'casualty'. Wallie, who had been walking across a parking lot towards our tent when the shooting erupted, was struck in the face by a small piece of flying debris or shrapnel, apparently emanating from one of the explosions occurring off in the distance. Though his injury was slight, barely breaking the skin, it was a foreboding of what was to come, as Wallie would be 'wounded' again later, while inside his room in the 'Tin Hut' at the Baghdad Police Academy.

Needless to say, there were a number of comments among those of us watching the battle, concerning 'how safe we were', as we had been told the preceding days, and how we 'shouldn't be concerned about not having weapons'. Once again we discovered that we had not been told the truth by those running the ICITAP program.

The gunfire finally subsided and then came to an end, but I'm sure that not many of us slept soundly, unsure if we might be the next target of what seemed to us to be an insurgent attack just a few hundred meters away. The next morning, Barney stopped by the palace and we told him of the battle. He was surprised not to have heard anything about it. His response was "You're kidding me?" We all assured him that it wasn't a matter for levity and that one of our group had actually been hit in the face by a piece of flying debris from one of the explosions.

We subsequently found out that the firefight we had witnessed had not actually been a firefight at all. We were told that a rocket from somewhere outside the Green Zone had been fired into the fortified area and had struck a Bradley Fighting Vehicle, parked near the courthouse building. The ammunition inside the Bradley had begun to 'cook off', giving the appearance of a firefight in the dark. Regardless of the cause, the entire incident was rather disconcerting to those of us who witnessed it, and we certainly let Barney have it about all the earlier assurances that we had been given that we didn't need weapons. I'm guessing a few of our group probably started to have second thoughts about what they had gotten themselves into.

There is one thing you simply never do to a cop—you don't try to bullshit him. Cops don't respond real well to bullshit being sent our way as a response to anything. By now, our feelings about the Adnan crowd were that all they knew how to do was to bullshit people. There was bad blood developing between us 'grunts', who were soon to be on the front lines at the various police academies around Iraq, and the people running the program back in the Green Zone. They were the typical REMs (Rear Echelon Motherfuckers, to use a military term), that every war has. There have always been people filling support positions back in the rear areas, and in the military there are about 10 REMs for every warfighter who is actually out there on the front lines doing the fighting, the bleeding, and the dying.

One of the common jokes we shared was at the expense of those self-appointed senior managers within the ICITAP program. Oftentimes you would walk into the Adnan Palace foyer and see senior ICITAP types standing around in groups of two or three, arms folded across their chests, appearing to be in high-level discussions about our project to bring Western democratic policing to Iraq. In fact, it was nothing more than a 'harrumphing' session.

It always reminded me of the Mel Brooks film *Blazing Saddles*, when Brooks played the character of Governor Le Petomane. I recall one scene in particular from the movie where Le Petomane and his aides are all standing around in the governor's office, arms folded across their chests while harrumphing to each other. One aide forgets to harrumph and Brooks walks over and says, "I didn't get a harrumph from you," to which the offender quickly harrumphs in reply. I always thought of that scene when I witnessed the pompous asses from the Green Zone who stood around in their little groups. Their lofty, high-level conversations were nothing more than attempts to impress each other with what was likely nothing more than pure bullshit. An exercise in 'Hey, look at me, I'm important'.

ICITAP had more official titles than one could shake a stick of TNT at. There was chief of staff, executive officer, regional director, regional investigations director, regional academy director, academy director, training director… and on and on and on. There were so many titles it was hard to keep track of them. We all became convinced that these positions were not necessarily given to the most qualified or the best leaders, but to those who got to Iraq first and laid a claim, or those who were the best at currying favor—the 'brown-nosers' to be more specific. Among our group of lowly instructors we had former police chiefs, senior detectives, GS-15s from federal agencies, who had overseen large staffs and budgets and who were obviously very well-qualified to hold senior positions within ICITAP, but they didn't get to Iraq first, so they were relegated to just being Iraqi police trainers.

In reviewing the careers of some of the senior managers, it was obvious that most of them had no more experience in leadership positions or senior law-enforcement management than any of those in my group. One individual in particular, Dane Borotsky, who had 'retired' as chief from a western state police department, was one of the most pompous of all of them. Dane passed himself off as some moral authority, thumping his bible in our faces and passing judgment on those of us who didn't share his religious beliefs. In fact, as we would later learn, Chief Dane had 'retired' from his last job at a fairly large police department under a cloud of sexual harassment allegations made by a female employee. He was not the paragon of virtue and moral authority that he portrayed himself as.

I've never had much use for hypocrites, and Dane certainly fit that description. He could regularly be found as close to any high-ranking military officer as he could get without actually being inside the guy's clothes with him. We used to joke that his nose was so far up some general's ass that if the general turned a sharp corner he'd break Dane off at the ankles. He was also a great 'harrumpher'.

Most of the other senior managers of ICITAP were so forgettable that I really can't remember names, only that they all fit the same general profile. In our group we had a real retired GS-15, not one of the phony GS-15 'equivalent' ICITAP employees, like the rank that was listed on our CAC cards. Dalma had served in a senior position with the U.S. Border Patrol and was a highly qualified individual. We also had senior-level agents from the Customs Service and the IRS, former police chiefs, and senior corrections officers as well, including Wallie, who had worked for a period of time at the White House.

Unfortunately, these talented and highly qualified individuals were relegated to positions as instructors of police cadets, instead of being given an opportunity to bring some real leadership and professionalism to the ICITAP program—a program that was in dire need of real leadership. When your program's slogan is 'Never have so many done so little for so much,' there is an obvious need for an overhaul.

The day after we received our weapons, we decided it was time to venture out on our own and do some exploring—within the Green Zone of course. Rather than just go to the PX and chow hall, we decided to check out the neighborhood around the Adnan Palace. What had become something of a rite of passage for everyone who served in

Baghdad, military and civilian alike, was to wander over to the Crossed Swords monument and parade boulevard to check them out and take some photos. Naturally, we all had to have our photo taken standing in the middle of the boulevard with the swords rising behind us. The monument consists of two arches, each formed by a pair of hands holding swords, rising across the boulevard and meeting in the middle. Descriptions do them no justice, you have to see them to understand how impressive they are.

We also walked about halfway down the boulevard to the large elevated stand, where Saddam and his senior leadership once stood to review the Iraqi troops parading past them. The viewing platform rose about 30 feet above the boulevard and I had to admit to a little bit of a funny feeling standing there, knowing that my feet probably were standing in the same place Saddam Hussein had once stood. Of course, that didn't stop us from all taking the obligatory photographs, standing where Saddam had fired his rifle into the air. Naturally, we all had to mimic that famous pose, as did every other American who came to Baghdad.

We also decided to walk over towards the zoo area and what was referred to as 'Memorial Park'. There were a couple of dusty old fighter jets parked there and a few other monuments of one sort or another. Everything was in a state of disrepair and looked very much neglected. After over 10 years of sanctions, it was easy to understand how things had fallen into this state.

While it felt good to get out of the Adnan compound, it was a little surreal walking around the Memorial Park area. We were very near the wall separating the Green Zone from 'Injun territory', and you never felt completely safe. Actually, considering the mortars and rockets that were regularly fired into the Green Zone, you never *were* completely safe.

Just before Christmas 2004, after a couple of weeks residing at the Adnan Palace tent, we were paid a visit by one of the staff and advised that we would finally be moving over to the Baghdad Police Academy the next day. Two from our group, Tommy and Daniel, were being assigned to the police academy at the Al Assad Air Base, about an hour's flight north of Baghdad. The Al Assad Academy was much smaller than the Baghdad one, and had a much smaller cadet population. There were several other smaller regional police academies spread out across Iraq. The one in Sulaymaniyah, up north in the Kurdish region of Iraq, was highly coveted by everyone. Compared to Baghdad and all the other parts of Iraq, the Kurdish area was relatively safe and peaceful. The Kurds were friendly towards Americans and one could actually walk the streets somewhat freely in 'Suly', which was certainly not possible anywhere else in the country.

We were also advised that there was going to be a Christmas party at the Baghdad Country Club, next to the Adnan Palace, that evening, and that we could pay $20 if we wanted to stay and join the fun, and then catch a later PSD over to the Baghdad Police Academy. I for one had had enough of the Adnan crowd, as well as living out of a duffle bag and a suitcase. I was more than ready to move on regardless of where it was, so I chose not to stay for the party. Stan and Ruby and a few others elected to attend the party, a decision they later regretted. According to Stan they were basically lost in the shuffle. The Adnan crowd spent the entire time currying favor with senior military officers and paid no attention to any of the people from our group. They described it as a stuffy affair and a total waste of time, and a waste of money. There wasn't much return on the $20 investment—no fun was had by all, at least not from our group.

CHAPTER 6

Into the 'Red Zone'

Those of us who heading to the academy the next day were told to be packed and ready to leave by PSD (Protective Security Detail) escort the following morning. Our PSD was staffed by South African contractors, who had been making this run back and forth to the academy for some time. They knew all the routes, including where the choke points and potential ambush sites were, and they were skilled and highly trained. We traveled in four-vehicle convoys of up-armored SUVs, with bullet-resistant glass that provided adequate protection against small-arms fire, but not much against an RPG or an IED. Note that I did not say 'bullet-proof glass', since the glass in our vehicles only withstood small-arms fire for a short period and would eventually deteriorate and give way.

As we couldn't all be taken over to the academy at one time, several trips would have to be made. These movements required a great deal of coordination, so as to avoid running into military patrols or other PSD movements if at all possible. Departure times, routes, and numbers of vehicles all had to be decided ahead of time. There was a lot of planning and coordination that went into these movements of personnel, and OPSEC (Operational Security) had to be foremost in mind when planning and coordinating any movements, usually keeping the details secret until the last possible moment before departure.

I was lucky enough to be in the first group selected to go and, truthfully, I could not wait to get out of the Adnan Palace. I had had enough of just sitting around doing nothing. Yeah the money was good, but it was time to get to work and finally do something to earn it.

Having been forewarned that access to alcohol was very limited at the academy, we decided to make one last tactical beer run to Café Napoli to stock up. We bought everything we could get our hands on and there was considerable consternation as to whether the escort vehicles taking us to the academy would have any room left for any passengers. Not that we were all a bunch of drunks, but we didn't know how long it might be before we could purchase a six-pack again, so we weren't taking any chances. Whether one agrees with it or not, our occasional alcohol consumption served as something of an escape from the drudgery as well as the horrors of war. It 'softened the edges' a little, and helped us to wind down after a day of work.

The next morning, when the PSD showed up, I loaded my luggage and gear into the SUV and we finally departed the palace. I thought to myself that if I ever set foot there again it would be too soon. The ride to the academy was only about three or four miles across the Tigris River, but it was right through the heart of Baghdad and out into the 'Red Zone'. Those few miles could make for a treacherous trip, as military patrols and civilian PSDs found out regularly when they were ambushed or hit by an IED.

Baghdad is hard to describe for someone who hasn't been there. Uniform sandy brown in color, the buildings are close together, making many of the streets narrow and congested. What was obvious was the years of neglect the city had experienced under more than 10 years of U.N. sanctions. Concrete barriers, sandbags, barbed wire, crossing gates, and armed guards were everywhere. Because of the insurgency and the level of violence, extra security precautions had to be taken by those Iraqis trying to run businesses within the war zone.

And there were derelict vehicles everywhere. Lots of derelict vehicles. They were either abandoned due to a lack of spare parts or they had just run out of miles and given up. Some had obviously blown up, with twisted and wrecked remnants all that was left. I smiled to myself as we passed by one store front along the way, which had a faded and weathered sign printed in English, advertising the 'Palm Springs Travel Agency'. From the looks of the store front, it didn't seem like it was thriving. In fact, it didn't look like it was even open for business as a travel agency, or anything else for that matter. And while Palm Springs might be a nice destination, I suspect there weren't many Iraqis using an agency to travel anywhere, much less to the United States at that time in history.

Empty stores fronts outnumbered the open shops on nearly every street that we drove down, making one wonder what Baghdad must have looked like when it was a thriving Middle Eastern city, before the 'shock and awe' aerial bombardment at the beginning of the Second Gulf War, that is. Not to mention the years of urban combat taking place on its streets since the American invasion, with the insurgency not just killing American soldiers but shooting up other Iraqis as well.

Street merchants on many sidewalks and street corners were selling all kinds of goods and wares, proving that there was still an economy going on in the middle of the war—clothes, handbags, supposedly designer jeans, counterfeit DVDs of first-run American movies, and all manner of electronics products. From a distance, as we drove by, the merchandise all looked pretty cheap and of poor quality. It was also common to see a gutted and skinned sheep hanging in the open air, sold by the slice, pound, or whatever portion you could afford, I guess. I wouldn't vouch for how fresh it might be, since it could be 130 degrees outside during the summer months, and here's a sheep hanging outside in the heat with flies and all manner of other insects buzzing around it. I once saw an Iraqi fishing in the Tigris, who caught a large fish and just threw it into a duffle bag he had with him. He continued to fish for a couple more hours, while the fish he had caught 'ripened' in the heat.

The traffic was heavy and it was basically every man for himself—there was no traffic control anywhere, really. With limited electricity in the city, what power was available wasn't used to run the traffic signals that stood at many street intersections. They just stood there looking blankly at you, having lost their purpose in life. Many had probably lost some of their parts as well—they were routinely stolen by Iraqis and repurposed.

There were Iraqi police on some of the streets but they didn't seem too interested in directing traffic. They seemed to be much more interested in looking over their shoulder. One can hardly blame them, Iraqi police were getting killed by the bushel every day by the insurgency. The terrorist

Abu Musab al Zarqawi had declared war on the Iraqi police and military, as well as the Americans. It's hard to imagine having any sense of safety just standing in one location for extended periods of time, with a huge target figuratively painted on one's back. It's understandable they might not feel real motivated to become a stationary target, directing traffic at an intersection or a roundabout, many of which were natural bottlenecks and consequently perfect locations for an insurgent attack.

With no traffic control, Iraqi drivers just forced their way through intersections any way they could, including driving up onto curbs and sidewalks if that way offered the path of least resistance. It was a free-for-all in 3,000-pound vehicles. Since I couldn't speak Arabic, I couldn't translate the things being yelled by the Iraqi drivers, but my best guess is that they were yelling things very similar to what American drivers do during rush hour back in the United States. The only difference was that most of these drivers were carrying AK-47s or some other weapon with them. The term 'road rage' took on a whole new meaning.

Traveling the narrow city streets, I remember quietly saying my prayers to myself throughout the trip. I just *knew* that there was an IED on some street we were driving down with my name written all over it. "Hail Mary full of grace," was repeated over and over for a while and then I switched to the Lord's Prayer, just for a change of pace. While I wasn't a particularly religious person, I figured it certainly couldn't hurt to ask for a little help.

As we turned one corner, I recall hearing the loud crack of a rifle, which sounded very close. I naturally jumped in my seat and clutched my M-4 a little closer. The driver yelled back from his driver's seat.

"Don't worry," he said. "That was friendly fire. Someone got a little too close!" Some Iraqi had driven too close to the convoy and had been scared off with a shot across the bow, to use a nautical term. The PSD convoys in Iraq always had the right of way, regardless of what any traffic signs might say. Since most signals didn't work anymore (apart from the short supply of electricity, much of the electrical infrastructure had been destroyed during the invasion and had not yet been repaired), most often it was who got to an intersection first that ruled the road. Most Iraqis have a pretty good understanding of the unwritten rules regarding

PSD or military convoys, and they kept their distance from any that was traveling by. Car horns won't get the message across as well as an automatic weapon being fired at you. Hot lead flying in your direction definitely gets your attention, and 'drive defensively' takes on a whole new meaning.

Convoy vehicles have signs affixed on the rear, written in both Arabic and English, warning people to stay back or risk being shot. Iraqis have learned to recognize these convoys from far away and most try to keep their distance. Terrorists have also learned to recognize these convoys. In fact we began to jokingly refer to them as 'bullet magnets', and convoys regularly came under attack from insurgents. In a PSD convoy you stood out in a crowd and attracted a lot of attention, most of it not good.

Attacks on convoys were a pretty regular occurrence in Baghdad and around Iraq. Insurgents had begun to recognize the various routes they would take and would set up ambushes accordingly. That's why the routes and times of travel were always varied, to try to keep the insurgents off their guard. Ambushes were usually quick and unexpected, very violent, and over before you had the chance to identify the shooters' locations and return fire.

As I mentioned already, some contract security companies in Baghdad had success using beat up, nondescript automobiles to transport VIPs around the city. For me, I preferred to have an armored SUV and well-trained former U.S. special operators or South African commando escorts wrapped around me when I ventured 'outside the wire'.

The South Africans who handled the PSD convoys to and from the academy had a pretty good record. They didn't barrel their way through traffic, forcing Iraqis off the road or pushing them out of the way as some other escorts did. Some of the PSD contract companies in Iraq had done little towards winning the hearts and minds of the Iraqi citizenry with their escort tactics. Yes, at times unusual maneuvers and very aggressive driving were necessary. But some PSDs expected Iraqis to stop on a dime when their convoy entered a roundabout or an intersection, and they didn't hesitate to take a shot at anyone who didn't stop quickly enough. They left in their wake many an irate Iraqi whose radiator had been shot up when maybe all he was doing was hurrying home with the family's groceries. And in a country still suffering from United Nations sanctions, getting a new radiator might not always be possible.

Unfortunately, there was so much money being thrown around by the U.S. government in Iraq that it had become reminiscent of the Old West. There were lots of 'cowboys' of different nationalities, running around with guns doing PSD and escort work, many of them probably one step away from a penal institution somewhere. Some companies were so 'fly by night' that there was little vetting of the people they hired. If you claimed to be some sort of former military commando, you were hired.

There wasn't much accountability on the part of the U.S. government at that time either. Little actual vetting of resumes was conducted, with many of the jobs being found and filled by word of mouth. If you heard about a job third-hand, and you had the name of someone, you could pretty much be guaranteed of getting a job escorting PSDs or providing perimeter security for a compound. Some also provided escort duty for truck convoys, which often came under attack. All of the FOBs (Forward Operating Bases) needed supplies to operate, and those supplies were usually brought in by semi-truck convoys. There were a lot of American truck drivers working in Iraq as part of these convoys. They made a decent salary compared to what they made in America, but nowhere near the salary levels of the escort guards. Yet what they were doing was just as hazardous, if not more so, and the service they provided was vital.

The Iraqi Provisional Authority had basically turned a blind eye to what was happening with some of the fly-by-night companies, allowing them to fill their pockets with American taxpayer money and then skip town, having done nothing really constructive or having even fulfilled their contract. It was such a dangerous and difficult environment to work in that some companies simply weren't able to complete construction or other projects. Some of the outfits providing security and escort contracts were among the worst offenders, unfortunately, and in many cases they left in a rush when one of their people killed an innocent Iraqi or got involved in other illegal activities. When so much money is being thrown around, the scam artists are sure to arrive and take advantage of a situation. That fact has been a part of human involvement in any endeavor since forever. And unfortunately for the American taxpayers, there wasn't a lot of accountability for much of the funding that was being provided in Iraq, at least during this early stage of our involvement. Sacks of money were literally sitting in offices being disbursed for supposedly legitimate reasons, though corruption certainly existed in many cases.

CHAPTER 7

Camp Shield

We departed the relative safety of the Green Zone, through what was called the Assassins Gate, and out into Baghdad proper. After a trip through the city streets, across the Tigris River, and through a couple of treacherous roundabouts (which were notorious for ambushes), we finally arrived at the Baghdad Police Academy without incident, though it had been a long time since I'd said so many prayers at one time, probably not since the last time I attended confession. I had saved up a lot of sins to atone for—believe me, I had a lot to answer for. Fortunately, my heathen ways had not been held against me during my ride to the academy, and no IEDs or ambushes took place. The rest of our group would follow over the next two days until we were all back together once more.

As we approached the academy entrance, you could see the blast walls, concertina wire, guard towers, and sandbags that were ever-present around U.S. and coalition compounds throughout Iraq. Off in the distance was a tall, odd-shaped building, which we soon learned was the Iraqi Ministry of the Interior headquarters building. Basically, it was shaped like a tall shoe box with a lid on the top, maybe 25 stories tall.

Since the Ministry of the Interior oversaw the Iraqi police force, it was a frequent target of mortar and rocket attacks, many of which flew right over the Baghdad Police Academy. Some didn't quite make it to the ministry and impacted within the academy compound instead. Or were they actually aimed at us? You never could tell really, because most of the 'mortars' used by the insurgents were mortars in name only—makeshift, homemade devices, which you could never really aim or tell for sure where your round was going to go.

Car bombings, rocket attacks, and small-arms fire were also fairly regular occurrences in and around the MOI Building, with the Baghdad Police Academy also a popular target for the insurgents, since we embodied social structure, law and order—all the things the insurgency was trying to undo.

During my trip to the academy, the only shot fired was the warning shot fired by our escort, but guns were at the ready throughout the ride just in case. We drove through the serpentine barriers at the entrance to the academy. The barriers formed a narrow lane that required you to drive back and forth, left and right, and at a slow speed. They were designed to give the armed guards plenty of time to react and shoot if you looked like you might be a suicide bomber barreling towards them. We came to a guard shack, where we stopped in order to be searched by security guards, as had been the case at the entrance to the Adnan Palace, and in fact at all entrances into the Green Zone. They 'mirrored' underneath the vehicles, and the driver had to pop the hood so they could look into and thoroughly inspect the engine compartment before we were allowed to proceed. We then pulled into a parking lot in front of a two-story building, which we later found was the main administrative building for the academy, called the 'AA building' because of the large letters 'AA' painted on it, likely standing for 'Academy Administration', although this was never made clear.

As we opened the doors to our SUVs and began to get unloaded, an American woman approached us and introduced herself as Carly. She had apparently been told of our arrival and was instructed to be our official welcoming committee. We were directed by Carly to get back into our vehicles and follow her as she led us through another small checkpoint and into another part of the compound, where we were to be billeted.

There were numerous military vehicles parked around in neat rows, and we stopped by a double-sized trailer-type building surrounded by the usual large concrete blast walls. The trailer was where we would be living for the foreseeable future. It was affectionately called the 'Tin Hut', since that's pretty much what it was made out of. Maybe 'Aluminum Hut' might have been more fitting, since the walls were pretty thin. It was also sometimes known as the 'hootch'.

The Tin Hut had just been vacated by the group of instructors who had preceded us to the academy, Carly among them. They had moved into a newly finished barracks nearby, constructed of concrete blocks covered in plaster (sand-colored naturally). The new barracks provided for single occupancy, unlike the Tin Hut, in which every room was home to two occupants. The new barracks also had better bath and shower facilities than we would have. Nearby, there were two other similar barracks under construction, but we were given no time-frame for when they would be finished. We unloaded again from our vehicles and approached the Tin Hut to lay claim to our rooms.

There was an older barracks area we called the 'Blue Lagoon', which was also was in the same part of the compound. Some of the very first instructors to come out to Baghdad were billeted there, and they also had single-occupancy rooms. The buildings were older and not in great shape, but having a room to yourself definitely made up for it.

Since the Tin Hut was surrounded by high concrete blast walls, you had to enter through an opening in the walls, then turn to your right after a few steps and basically backtrack until you reached the entrance. There were 16 rooms, eight on each side of a central, very wide space that ran the length of the trailer. Each room was not much larger than a good-sized walk-in closet. Two people were assigned to each room, which contained a couple of beds, two wall lockers, a TV, fridge, and a desk. I drew Ted as my roommate and we selected a room right next to one of the two bathroom facilities in the trailer, which were located across from each other mid-way down.

I thought the convenience of the bathrooms was a good idea, but I found out later that we had made a mistake. Water had a tendency to leak in under the wall separating our room from the bathroom and showers. 'Leak' is probably not an accurate word. 'Pour would be more appropriate. We were also subject to the noise emanating through the thin metal walls on both sides of us—the noise from those singing in the shower, as well as the more personal sounds emanating from someone using the toilet. As with everyone else except those on the ends of the hut, we also had noise coming from the room on the other side of ours.

The Tin Hut quickly filled up with our group, each of them pairing up and taking one of the rooms. A couple of the rooms were already occupied by some instructors who were getting ready to leave the country and had therefore not moved into the new barracks. The bottom line is that we had more than 30 people living in a space designed for about 16. And that is being generous. Packed in like sardines was an understatement.

As soon as you walked into our room, Ted's bed was to your left running half the length of the room, then came the walk lockers separating Ted's part of the room from mine. My bed was up against the far exterior wall and set cross-ways in the back of the room.

Roommates Mitch and Dudley ('the Pillsbury Dough Boy') had the room on the other side of the showers. Theirs was not a marriage made in heaven. Mitch was a former police officer from Texas and Dudley had apparently at one point been a small-town police officer for a few years in Colorado. Dudley had gone on to be a school teacher for much longer in his career. When you looked at Dudley, 'school teacher' is what came to mind. Either that or maybe 'florist', but 'police officer' was the last thing you would think of. Actually, Dudley resembled the Pillsbury Dough Boy far more than he did a school teacher. A Texas cop and the Pillsbury Dough Boy, the duo were destined for hard times.

There were two females living in the Tin Hut—Ruby, who would share a room with her husband Stan, and a holdover named Krista. The ladies laid claim to one of the bathroom/showers midway down the trailer, across from the one shared by the rest of us males. The remaining couple dozen of us men had to share three showers and three toilets, while the two women had three toilets and three showers between them. Something didn't quite seem fair, but these were the conditions we were faced with so we made the best of it.

At one point I tried to convince the gals to allow us to share their bathroom, we could put a sign on the door letting anyone know there was a male inside, and vice versa for females. They didn't go for it. In fact that would be another understatement, they both vehemently refused. I guess they didn't want a bunch of guys using their toilets and forgetting to lift the seat up, or return it to its original position after finishing. I can't really say I blamed them, if you've seen a men's bathroom before.

After dropping off our gear, we stepped back outside and were met by a guy named Arnie, a friend of Carly's who had also come over to welcome us. At first, Arnie seemed like a decent sort of fellow, but we subsequently found out that he represented the epitome of the term 'brown-noser'. Arnie was all about Arnie—he was great at currying favor with whomever he thought might benefit him.

Arnie, his friend Carly, and another gal named Katherine (and another named LaDonna who was back home in the States on leave when we arrived), would turn out to be a nightmare for me personally, and a pain in the ass for all of us. All four were a perfect example of how desperate the government was to get anyone to go to Iraq and teach Iraqi police cadets. None of the four had served as police officers for any length of time, so their qualifications to teach cadets were in serious question. On top of that, none of them had the right temperament to be working and living in a war zone, where people were fighting and dying daily, and where they might be called upon to watch your back or fight alongside you in a jam. Not a comforting thought.

Arnie's biggest complaint centered on the lack of toilet paper in the 'hootch', and that he had to have family mail him rolls from back home. Over time, and after getting to know these individuals and witnessing some of their really juvenile antics, I could not understand how someone could act so immaturely in the middle of a war zone. It was certainly not the place for people to act like little kids. Watching them would have been amusing if it wasn't such a dangerous environment, where lives were at stake. They played cliquish little games that you would have thought had been left behind in high school years earlier. They were definitely an unwanted annoyance, but one that could be navigated through once you knew what they were.

To his credit, Arnie volunteered to give us the nickel tour of the FOB, showing us the military chow hall, laundry, dispensary, and the very small PX run by the 1st Cavalry Division troops assigned to the base. The PX consisted of one small room inside a small building, and had a few electronic items, coffee, some canned goods, chips, candy bars, and prepackaged small food items. And microwave popcorn! It was pretty meager pickings really, but at least it was something. It was not even close to the inventory of the PX back in the Green Zone. The soldier responsible for running it had troops pick up items for him during trips to the Green Zone or to Camp Cuervo, which was several miles away. He would then stock his little PX with whatever they had been able to gather up.

FOB Shield, as it was called, was broken up into two halves. One half housed troops from the 1st Cavalry Division, while the other half included the billeting area for the ICITAP instructors. The Baghdad Police Academy Headquarters in the 'AA' building and the actual academy training areas (including the classrooms, firearms range, and cadet billeting area) were separated from us by high T-walls and manned guard towers.

Leaving the academy side of the FOB where we lived, and entering the 1st Cavalry Division side, one had to go through another checkpoint staffed by 1st Cav soldiers. There were 'gun-clearing barrels' located at the checkpoint, and before you could proceed into the 1st Cav side you had to clear your weapons. A clearing barrel was nothing more than a 50-gallon metal drum cut in half and filled with sand or dirt. You would hold your weapon over the barrel, muzzle pointed at the dirt, and eject any ammunition that was loaded into the chamber. Even if you didn't have any ammunition loaded you still had to rack the weapon's action back, so that the checkpoint guard could see that your weapon was clear and unloaded. This was not something cops were very fond of, since as police officers in the U.S. it could have been suicide to walk around with an unloaded weapon. You simply didn't have time to load a magazine into your 9mm, rack in a round, and then engage a bad guy in an emergency. He would have been able to empty his gun into you before you were able to even withdraw your magazine from its pouch on your gun belt.

Old habits die hard, especially for cops, and we complained to the military about this requirement, but to no avail. We all went through the routine of unholstering our guns and clearing them, then proceeding through the checkpoint and into the 1st Cav area. Once inside, when no one was watching, most of us would then immediately reload at least one round into the chamber of our 9mm. The army guys were none the wiser and it at least gave us a sense of comfort, knowing we'd be able to get one round off in an emergency. The 1st Cavalry unit's First Sergeant used to wander around the FOB and if he saw a weapon with the magazine inserted, he'd call you out on it and make you remove it and go to the nearest clearing barrel. So we'd put the magazine with the rest of the rounds into its pouch on our belt and manage with just the single round in the chamber. The First Sergeant wasn't really fond of us anyway. I think there was a little jealousy on his part that we were all making a lot of money, while he was only getting his army pay, but that wasn't our fault. A great many of us were veterans and had done our time years earlier, making a hell of a lot less than soldiers did in 2004.

The 1st Cav side of FOB Shield was a pretty large area. I'm not certain of the acreage but the best description I can provide is that it was the size of a dozen football fields at least, though not all of it had structures on it or was anything more than vacant areas. Way off in the distance you could see a fairly good-sized and oddly shaped structure. It resembled a gymnasium or something like that from a distance. We found out later that it was the Olympic swimming and diving facility that Saddam had constructed for his failed attempt to attract the Olympic Games to Baghdad some years before. To the best of my knowledge, it was abandoned and unused—just a large, empty monument to Saddam's visions of grandeur.

There were quite a few other buildings being used by the 1st Cav, some to billet troops and others housing various logistics and admin offices. They had a small MWR (Morale, Welfare and Recreation) facility, where soldiers could make phone calls home and relax a little after duty. There was a collection of board games, decks of cards, a TV and some DVD movies, but not a whole lot else. It was pretty spartan in comparison to what was offered at MWRs on the larger bases in Iraq, but it provided a diversion and helped break the monotony of life in Baghdad for the GIs. I visited it once just to check it out and never returned.

There was also a small local vendor area, where Iraqis who had been vetted could enter FOB Shield and offer trinkets, crafts, and other souvenirs to anyone interested. Considering the high unemployment rate in Baghdad, and the American goal of winning hearts and minds, it was decided on as official U.S. government policy to try to accommodate these small vendors, giving them a place to sell their wares and make a few bucks to provide for their families. Most likely they were serving two masters, selling crap to the soldiers and also providing intelligence to the insurgency.

The 1st Cav chow hall, or DFAC (Dining Facility), was a fairly large dining area and laid out a pretty good spread of food for each meal. You certainly could not complain about the food we had, at least until the 1st Cav packed up, moved out, and took their chow hall with them. When that happened, the academy made preparations ahead of time to have an Iraqi catering company come in and feed us temporarily until a new military chow hall could be set up.

The tour of the FOB didn't take long and once it was over, Arnie offered to take us down to the academy classroom area, which I declined to visit. It was a long walk and I didn't feel like trudging down there only to have to walk back. After 10 minutes with Arnie it had become clear to me that he suffered from his own delusions of grandeur anyway, and he enjoyed very much hearing himself talk about his vast, extensive experience in Iraq. Arnie had gotten there one month before us so his experience wasn't really that vast.

As for his police experience, we found out that Arnie had in fact served as an officer for a few years somewhere back in the States, but he had left law enforcement for a job with Lowes or Home Depot, checking receipts as you leave the store—a much more challenging career. Like many others, when the lure of big money appeared he jumped at the chance of coming to Iraq to cash in. I can't really blame him for that, that's pretty much why we were all there, at least initially. With Carly, Katherine, and LaDonna, he had found kindred souls with whom he could commune and gossip. He had found his little clique of like-minded individuals.

After separating from Arnie and the others, I returned to the little PX where I had seen a small microwave oven for sale. It was the only one there so I immediately purchased it for $40. It was a wise decision, but it had a downside as well. My microwave quickly became a 'community microwave', with people stopping by my room to cook popcorn, soups, and anything else that would fit inside of it. I didn't really mind though,

I figured we were all in this together so I might as well pitch in where I could. If my microwave was more popular than I was, that was fine with me, but for that reason alone I became a very popular guy in the Tin Hut. The chow hall provided some excellent meals, but nothing made you forget about the war more than a hot bag of microwave popcorn. Especially after the chow hall would close down and stop serving meals for the night. If those evening munchies hit you, my microwave and a packet of popcorn was the perfect answer.

With the tour and my shopping spree at the PX over, I went back to my room and started to unpack my gear and try to get settled in. Unfortunately for me, Ted took up way more room than I did with his numerous duffle bags of tactical crap. I crammed my stuff into one corner of the room, and basically gave 'Tackleberry' two thirds of the space for his stuff. It still wasn't enough. For the next three nights I got very little sleep, as Ted stayed up into the wee hours of the morning unpacking, re-packing, and then unpacking all of his duffle bags. He couldn't seem to get his stuff to fit into the space available—not surprising considering he had even packed a small electric fan inside one of his duffle bags, which he was able to mount on the wall of the room. I kept waiting for the kitchen sink to appear out of one of his bags.

Finally, I said something to Ted about his nocturnal activities and asked if he could get his gear unpacked and stowed away or at least do it during the daytime so as not to keep me awake all night. Ted apologized and finally got settled in, though he continued to rummage through his duffle bags constantly, pulling more surprises out on a regular basis.

One thing about Ted which I always found humorous was his tendency to be super-polite. Ted was so formal and courteous that it made you uncomfortable. There's nothing wrong with being courteous, but when someone apologizes for something when you were the culprit, it makes you wonder. But Ted was living a dream—he was so happy to be where he was in Iraq. He dressed every day in all of his tactical gear, when the rest of us rarely wore our body armor or carried our M-4s. Ted had never served in the military, so now he was getting the chance to play 'army' for real. He immediately volunteered to be a firearms instructor and teach the cadets how to shoot properly. In fairness, by all indications

Ted was a very good shot and he turned out to be a very patient and good firearms instructor for the cadets.

And right away Ted began to learn Arabic. This was admirable, but it sometimes caused consternation for the rest of us when he'd try out his language skills and talk to us in Arabic. We'd have to bust his chops and tell him to switch back to English. I used to say, "I don't speak Arabic, don't want to learn to speak Arabic, and if you want to talk to me then speak English instead of babbling to me in Arabic all the time." It was my version of the 'ugly American' I guess. I was never really good with foreign languages and didn't see the need to learn Arabic since we had very good Iraqi translators assigned to us anyway.

The next day came and we were ushered into a conference room in the AA building for a series of briefings. We were welcomed by a Scottish policeman named Hitchins, who was the academy's assistant director. The director, Malcolm (another Scotsman), was away on a visit home. Hitchins seemed to be a decent and friendly enough guy. It was also during these briefings that we met for the first time the very forgettable 'Halleluiah Mack'. Halleluiah Mack had been at the academy for about a month more than us. His law-enforcement career was limited to serving as an 'investigator' in a corrections department back in the States. Basically, he investigated crimes that were committed inside of a prison. Not a typical patrol officer working the streets and responding to calls for service. Mack loved to use the phrase 'Slap leather' whenever talking shop. Not many corrections officers back in the States get into running gun battles where they have to 'slap leather', but Mack certainly liked to use the phrase.

Mack had either been selected, or more likely volunteered, to give one of the briefings we were to hear that morning. He discussed some of the challenges of teaching the Iraqi cadets. His experience was limited, but to hear him talk you would have thought he'd been there for years.

"These Iraqis, they're all thieves and liars and can't be trusted" he said during his monologue. "They'll steal anything if you turn your back on them. They're dirty and filthy too."

In the room with us were a number of Iraqi translators standing off to the side. They worked at the academy, translating for the American instructors and administrators. I found it rather embarrassing and insulting the way Mack went on and on about how the Iraqi cadets were dirty, thieving, lying, cheating people, and you had to watch them like a hawk. How he gained so much experience and knowledge in just one month, and why he'd been picked to participate in the briefing, I'm not sure, but my guess is he was also a brown-noser like Arnie, and had weaseled his way into giving a briefing by currying favor.

Were I not so new and unsure of my footing I would have gotten up and walked out of the room right then and there. I really took umbrage at the comments Mack was making, particularly with Iraqis standing right there in the room with us. It was insulting and as far as I was concerned Mack was much more the epitome of the 'ugly American' than I ever was for not wanting to learn Arabic. At least I didn't bad mouth and insult the Iraqis with them standing right there in the room with us.

What was truly ironic, was that at the end of his briefing Mack shared with us that he was a Christian and he invited us all to attend religious services with him, and also a Wednesday night bible study that he hosted. Apparently, he served as something of an 'elder' with a church group on the FOB. So after spending an hour insulting his fellow man, he then tells us what a good Christian he is and invites us to church. I consider myself a Christian as well, though some may call me a heathen since I haven't attended a formal church service church in a long time—it's that lightning bolt thing, it scares me—but in my earlier years, while regularly attending church, I do not recall ever hearing that it was the Christian thing to do to insult and demean other people. We all agreed that Halleluiah Mack was a real piece of work and someone to keep your distance from.

After our briefing with Mack it was back to the 'hootch' with nothing to do. The only difference from our routine at the Adnan Palace was our new location. The routine didn't vary much for the next several days, but one interesting aspect of living in the Tin Hut was the daily cleaning ritual performed by some local Iraqis who worked in the compound. They would come into the main central corridor of the Tin Hut in order to clean the floor, which was warped so badly it moved when you walked across it. Tiles were also missing and many others were loose and just laying on top of the floor, not really glued down or attached in any way. The cleaning crew would come in with buckets of water—who knew where it came from, or what diseases it might carry—and they would just throw the water out across the floor. Buckets and buckets of soapy water. They'd then get busy with their mops and squeegees, moving the water around and pushing it through the door onto the ground outside. Some of the water escaped through holes in the floor no doubt. This was probably why the floor was so warped in the first place—it had become waterlogged after repeated soakings by the cleaning crew. Every day it was the same routine. They'd come in, throw several buckets of soapy water on the floor, mop it up and then leave. The floor was warped and weakened by the constant dampness, and we were never sure that we wouldn't fall right through one day as we walked across it.

Finally, after several days of doing nothing, we were advised that a new class would be starting and the next day we were told to report to a large gymnasium near the rear gate of the academy side of the compound, off Palestine Street. Palestine Street ran right into the heart of Sadr City, which was basically a ghetto and a hotbed of insurgent activity. That evening, while sitting outside the Tin Hut, we chatted amongst ourselves about what to expect the next day. Some of us were apprehensive, others relaxed and unconcerned, but we were all anxious to finally have something to do and get started. You can only sit around and do nothing for so long before you start to get a little agitated, and it also sets up the opportunity for conflicts to develop.

While our group got along really well for the most part, those that had preceded us and were already at the Academy when we arrived were less than friendly overall. It was a pretty cliquish environment. We all basically kept to ourselves within our little groups and didn't intermingle much.

Saddam Hussein's viewing platform at the Boulevard of the Swords monument.

The 'AA' Administration Building at the Baghdad Police Academy.

The Iraqi Ministry of the Interior, next to the Baghdad Police Academy.

The author and high-stakes poker at the Baghdad Police Academy.

The pool behind Saddam Hussein's palace in the Green Zone.

Cadets on the march.

Cadets lined up for class.

Inside the tent at the Adnan Palace.

Tents outside the Adnan Palace.

The author 'in the shadow of the swords'.

A Tahitian 'Commando' at the Baghdad Police Academy.

The 'Blue Lagoon' at the Baghdad Police Academy.

Wiffle Ball Champs.

Sitting around the fire pit outside the Tin Hut at the Baghdad Police Academy.

Saying goodbye.

The Tin Hut surrounded by blast walls.

An explosion near the Ministry of Oil.

Inside the Green Zone, heading to the bank to cash a check.

Iraqi Police Cadets.

A 'tactical beer run'.

Adnan Palace tents.   Near Adnan Palace and swords.

Saddam's Green Zone palace.

Monument to the Martyrs.

Hard at work in the Tin Hut.

Colleagues in front of the 'Del Wilber Memorial Bar' at the Baghdad Police Academy.

CHAPTER 8

Personalities

There were lots of interesting personalities who made up the academy instructor staff, and some of them had no business being there at all. Carly apparently possessed no real prior law-enforcement experience, and had only been a school teacher back in the States. The one thing she apparently did have was a friendship with someone senior at the contracting company that provided instructors for the program. It appears her lack of experience as a police officer was overlooked and she was hired based on her experience as a teacher, and being a friend of somebody in a position of power. It was all about who she knew, not what she knew. Since the actual classroom curriculum and training material was already prepared, all she really had to do was follow the course material. She would be teamed up with another instructor anyway, who presumably had actual police experience, so I guess they figured that would take care of any deficiencies she had on the law-enforcement side. I'm sure that the military and the Iraqis never knew that she was not an experienced police officer, or she would not have been allowed to participate, and she would have missed out on all the big money. But I have to say that watching her walk around with a 9mm pistol strapped to her hip was a little disconcerting, to say the least. Her behavior also called into question her being part of the program. She reminded me of a young girl in high school, immature and subject to playing little games—certainly not what is needed in the middle of a war zone.

Katherine was an older women who apparently had served in a corrections position back in America. Though not really a police officer, at the time they were accepting corrections officers to teach at the police academy. In the early stages of the war and the reconstruction efforts, they had difficulty getting experienced police officers to come over to Iraq, so they made exceptions. Katherine apparently was one of those exceptions. She and Carly were buddies, and even though Katherine was older, she also played the little games right along with Carly. Arnie I have already talked about, so suffice it to say that he fit in really well with Carly and Katherine's little clique. Then there was LaDonna, who had been home on leave when I arrived. Apparently she had been originally selected to fill the 'HR' position that I would eventually take over, but she had really made no effort to get it up and running before departing for her visit to the States. That's why the academy director and assistant director decided to look elsewhere, which led to me eventually being selected. That decision ruffled some feathers in the Carly, Katherine, Arnie, and LaDonna clique, as they all viewed me as a usurper.

Then there was 'Surfer Boy'. The senior firearms instructor was called Surfer Boy due to his full wavy hair and well-cultivated tan. He looked like he was right off of Venice Beach in California. He was also what we would call a 'major league cock hound', chasing any 'skirt' that happened to show up at the academy. We received visitors often from the Green Zone, and many of the visits included females, either military or civilian, as part of the group. Surfer Boy could always be found nearby, offering his services as a guide whenever one of these visits occurred. He was also known as 'missing in action' at all other times, when there were no visitors that included females. He was a senior firearms instructor, though the instructors working with the students rarely saw him. In fact, he was really difficult to locate at any time. As with many of the other 'Triple C' instructors (Train the Trainer), Surfer Boy disappeared for days on end. He simply couldn't be located unless you happened to see him at the chow hall.

Sarah and Sandy were two older sisters who had been police officers back in America for a few years. They were a couple of nice ladies, and although I wasn't sure when I first met them that they belonged in the middle of Baghdad, they would prove me wrong. Sarah approached me one day after I had been 'promoted', just after she arrived at the academy, asking if I could help get her sister Sandy out there. Sarah had gotten to Iraq first and Sandy was going to follow her once she took care of some personal business back home. I remember Sarah coming to me and asking, "Del, is there anything you can do to get my sister assigned here to the Baghdad Academy? We'd like to be together if we can, but they wouldn't make any promises over in the Green Zone." I told her that I also couldn't make any promises, but I would see what I could do. I made a couple of calls and ultimately was able to arrange for Sandy to get assigned to Baghdad instead of one of the outlying academies. They were both very appreciative. It was kind of fun watching them bicker back and forth at each other, as sisters often do. Sarah and Sandy would also be part of our wiffle ball team when we took on the military, and they performed admirably. They were more than willing to pitch in and help whenever asked.

Bryan LeFave was an interesting individual. A 'snake in the grass' would be a more apt description of him—he was definitely someone not to turn your back on. While he smiled all the time, and acted as though he was your good friend, he was always out to curry favor with the bosses and would knife you in the back in a heartbeat if it played to his benefit. He lived with the Blue Lagoon crowd and put on the appearance of being everyone's friend, but he was never one to trust. You could never be sure if his smile was sincere, or if he was contemplating your demise.

One of the things he liked to do was greet all new instructors when they arrived and prank them about bringing alcohol to the academy in violation of the military's General Order No. 1. He would meet the new arrivals and immediately go into his shtick, asking them in a very official and stern voice, "Have any of you brought any alcohol along with you from the Green Zone? You need to understand that it is against General Order No. 1. No alcohol is allowed on Iraqi military installations." Bryan would then offer them amnesty if they stepped forward and turned their alcohol over to him. Usually the convoys would be full of alcohol because they had been forewarned to stock up. The new arrivals would all sheepishly admit to having alcohol and reluctantly start to gather it up from the pile of luggage on the ground behind them. Bryan would play the joke for a few minutes and then let them know he was just kidding. He pulled the same scam on every group.

Halleluiah Mack's true character came out on one occasion. A fairly large group of 15 or 20 new instructors arrived, including two who were African American. The new group seemed to be fairly decent guys and we welcomed them to our nightly gathering around the fire pit, to help them feel at home. Since there were no cadets for them to teach at that moment, there really wasn't much for them to do but kill time any way they could. They were billeted in some very old barracks buildings on the 1st Cav side of the FOB, some of which didn't even have windows or doors. I don't believe there was even electricity hooked up to the building—austere doesn't even come close to describing these living conditions. It was intended that these would be short-term, temporary lodgings, only for a day or two at the most. Even at that I thought it was pretty poor treatment to send these new people over the academy when we didn't have a proper place for them to stay, but it was typical of ICITAP in Iraq—not a lot of planning or coordination. The goal was to just get people somewhere so they weren't hanging around the Adnan Palace and getting in the way.

One day, Halleluiah Mack approached me as I was walking across the compound and he seemed agitated. As he got near me he said, "You know those two new black instructors?" I responded, "Yeah, what about them?" I didn't really know them as they had just gotten to the academy and I hadn't had the chance to get better acquainted with them, or really any of the new group as of yet. But Mack went on to say "Well, they're not doing anything. Just sitting around." This struck me as a pretty curious comment since there was nothing for them to be doing. Everybody was 'just sitting around'. There was no class to teach, nor were there any other duties they were assigned to do. It wasn't an ideal situation, but that was the way it was at that moment. Mack kind of shook his head and then walked away muttering to himself, pulling a small notebook from his shirt pocket and scribbling away. It was pretty apparent to me from his comments and actions that there was a tinge of racism involved in the exchange. It didn't seem to occur to him that there was a bunch of white instructors who also were just sitting around. At least he didn't mention 'slapping leather' this time.

Anyway, I never had the occasion to mention it to the two new officers. It wouldn't have served any purpose anyway, other than to cause disruption or bad feelings, which we simply didn't need at the time. I did mention it to Baghdad Boob when we were sitting around the fire pit one evening and he kind of shrugged, just acknowledging it. He knew as well as I did that Halleluiah Mack was a strange individual.

Tackleberry was also unique. As my roommate, I got to know him fairly well. he was polite and friendly, but just a little squirrelly. Everywhere he went on the academy grounds he looked like he was ready for battle to break out at any minute. As I mentioned previously, he was always super polite when talking with people, in the kind of way that often made you feel a little bit uncomfortable, but I never thought there was any ulterior motive on his part. He was just that way.

Baghdad Boob was a great guy. I was always reminded of the character Oddball from the movie *Kelly's Heroes*. And I mean that as a compliment. Bob was just easygoing and cool. He sat around the fire pit at night and rarely said much, but when he did it was usually hilarious. He'd just sip on a Jack and Coke and take everything in. The unofficial 'camp philosopher', Bob never got upset about anything, he just went with the flow, wherever it took him. I guess living near the beach back home in South Carolina had instilled something of a free-spirit outlook in him.

Wallie was a good guy as well, very responsible and dedicated. He, along with most of the others of our group, was great to work with. Wallie also is the only one of us who got wounded in Iraq. Most everyone, in fact, with the exceptions noted, were pretty decent people. Our group worked well together and got along very well most of the time.

Stan and Ruby were pretty nice people. The best description I can give for Stan is that he was steady and unflappable. Like Baghdad Boob, he also pretty much took things in his stride. He had a good sense of humor and was very easy to get along with. Ruby, Stan's wife, was a nice gal as well and came across as a good team player. Unfortunately for her, she was approached early on by the Carly-Arnie-Katherine clique, who were looking for a new recruit to their little gang. When Ruby showed no interest in joining in their little schemes then she too became immediately ostracized by them.

Dudley, the 'Pillsbury Dough Boy', was a rather curious individual. Chubby and pudgy, he really did resemble the character you saw in the TV ads selling biscuits. And from the looks of him, he had consumed his fair share of biscuits over the years. He was also a rather timid individual, and it was difficult to picture him as a police officer back in the States. Certainly not in the ghetto, where I had spent much of my career—he would have gotten chewed up and spit out very quickly. Every night, his roommate Mitch told us that he would put little booties on his feet as he settled in for the evening. Then he would lay there on his bed and just jabber away as Mitch was trying to get to sleep. He would also pry into Mitch's business, including hovering over Mitch's shoulder as he opened a care package, filled with goodies that had been sent from loved ones back home.

The academy director, Malcolm, was a pretty decent guy, though it was really hard to tell for sure since he spoke with a very heavy Scottish accent. I almost felt like I needed a translator to understand him as much as I needed one to understand the Iraqis. His No. 2, Hitchins, was also easy to get along with, and Jane, a third member of the Scottish police who had been sent to the academy, was also nice, although I never had much contact with her. At least, not as much as most of us men would have liked. Her sweaters fit her really, really well, if you get my drift. In fact the guys in our group would sit around our campfire at night and concoct schemes on how we might get her to take her shirt off.

My initial partner in the classroom, Kenny, had come over to Iraq with Stan and Ruby. They had all worked in the same department back in the States and had decided to go on this great adventure together. Kenny was also a decent guy, and we worked together in the classroom very well, following each other's lead with ease. He was very easy to get along with.

On one occasion, after I had taken on the HR manager role at the academy, I decided to apply for one of the many titled positions with ICITAP that were spread around Baghdad and the rest of the country. It wasn't so much that I wanted one of those positions, I was pretty content with staying at the Baghdad Academy working with a good group of people, and if you made a change you never knew what you might end up with. The grass isn't always greener, as they say. But applying for a new position would offer an opportunity to go over to the Green Zone, where I could visit the PX and make a tactical beer run to the Napoli Café. I would take orders from everyone else and help them stock up their supply of adult beverages for the long days ahead.

On the day I was scheduled to head over to the Green Zone, the PSD showed up and I geared up with my body armor, Kevlar helmet, and M-4. I loaded up into the SUV for the trip, bringing only a small bag with the bare essentials for the overnight stay at the tent at the Adnan Palace. Our trip through the streets of Baghdad over to the Green Zone was uneventful, and after arriving at the palace I went into the visitor tent, found a cot, and dropped my gear off.

I noticed right away that the tent was nearly full. There was a bunch of new instructors staying in the tent, awaiting assignment. Most of them likely would be going to the Baghdad Police Academy. I greeted the few who were seated around the table in the center of the tent, next to where the TV and refrigerator were located. When they found out where I had come from, they started to ask questions, and it was clear the BPA was where most of them had been told they were headed. I tried to answer whatever questions they threw my way.

My interview wasn't scheduled until the next morning, so I relaxed for a bit and then grabbed a vehicle to head over to the PX and see if there was anything new worth buying. At Café Napoli I filled out all the orders that had been given to me by colleagues before I left. It was not a major order this time, and the visit was short and completed without incident. I decided to stop by one of the military chow halls to grab some lunch before heading back to the Adnan Palace. Once again I had a fitful night in the tent. With so many people around, half of them snoring like a freight train, it certainly wasn't an environment conducive to a good night's sleep.

The next morning I got up and showered and then went to meet the person conducting the interview at the palace. The interview itself was short, with the interviewer seeming to be pretty distracted, as though he was just going through the motions. I got the distinct impression that someone had already been selected for the position, since it was a Green Zone job, and that was fine with me since I wasn't really interested in leaving the Baghdad Police Academy anyway. The job had probably been promised to one of the Green Zone clique, but HR rules insisted it had to be officially posted and interviews conducted.

After my interview, I made my way back to the Adnan Palace in order to await my PSD that afternoon to take me back to the academy. While I was killing time in the tent, I noticed that a case of Corona Beer, which I had purchased at Café' Napoli, was missing. It had either walked off on its own, or been spirited away by one of my new 'roommates' in the tent. Since it made no sense to try to figure out who stole it (no one was ever going to admit to it), I just decided to let it drop. There had never been an issue with things 'walking off' with our group, so the thought never occurred to me that anything I left in the tent might disappear. Oh well, lesson learned.

The ride back to the academy that afternoon went smoothly, with no real issues along the way. As we approached one of the notorious roundabouts, I did hear a couple of gunshots that sounded pretty close, but I couldn't tell if they were directed at us or if they were just 'happy fire'. It always got your attention though, since you couldn't be sure whether or not the first shot or two that you heard was going to be followed up by a full-fledged ambush.

Arriving at the academy, our PSD made it through the serpentine barriers and obstacles and entered the compound, where it came to a stop at the usual place. I saw my buddies seated around the fire pit, already gathered for the nightly pre-chow ritual of chatting, talking about the day's events, sharing news from home or just good-natured ribbing, which would be repeated that evening after chow. After unloading my gear and the supplies from Café Napoli, and once again thanking the PSD guys for getting me back home safely, I walked up to the group at the fire pit.

"So how'd your interview go?" said Jimmy Two Dogs.

"Turned down again," I replied. "There's no justice."

This was greeted by laughter from the group. I pointed over to the cases of beer and a couple of bottles of booze, piled up on the parking lot where I had been dropped off by the PSD, and said, "Need some help here." Everyone jumped up and headed over to help with the supplies. There were looks of approval as they walked away with their arms full, content to know that they'd be able to have a drink or two in the evenings for as long as this load of supplies held out—hopefully at least until the next trip to the Green Zone. I like to think that everyone was just a little relieved that I hadn't taken a job and abandoned them to their fate at the academy. At least while I was there with them, they knew they had someone in management who gave a damn about them and would look out for their interests.

There were many other instructors who passed through the academy, some staying longer than others, and some much less memorable than the ones I have mentioned. The ones I've highlighted either had a significant impact on me personally, or they were typical of the kind of individuals who were working at the Baghdad Police Academy. For being willing to put their lives at risk and accept the challenge, they all deserve some thanks, especially from the U.S. government.

CHAPTER 9

The Tin Hut and Cookies From Home

I've mentioned the Tin Hut quite a bit, so maybe now would be the appropriate time to give a little more attention to it.

There were three showers available for the men, as mentioned—three showers for over 30 of us. The showers had flimsy curtains held in place by a curtain rod. Depending on your point of view, the curtains were either three inches too short or the rods were mounted three inches too high. Water would spray out onto the floor through the gap between the shower curtain and the floor of every shower stall. Sometimes the water collected an inch or so deep on the floor outside the showers. There was a squeegee conveniently placed inside the room in order to mop out the shower after using it, to try and keep the water down to somewhat manageable levels. At least there wasn't a life preserver hanging on the wall. The Tin Hut had acquired the nickname of 'Camp Swampy', very likely based on the showers and the practices of the Iraqi janitors, who poured their buckets of soapy water all over the place every day.

Privacy in the three toilets inside the shower room was non-existent. There were folding plastic doors, which had runner guides mounted on the top of the stall opening. These doors were barely hanging from a single hinge on one side of the opening. One door had no hinges at all, it would simply lay up against you as you sat there, thinking deep thoughts. Sometimes while you were seated doing your business, the door would come loose and end up dropping into your lap.

On the tank above the toilet, the janitors would place three rolls of toilet paper every day. The rolls were small compared to American standards, and we only got three in each stall for over 30 men, making just nine rolls total each day. And this definitely wasn't the kind of toilet paper we were accustomed to in America. It was not made for comfort. It was thicker paper and it rolled around the cardboard core only a couple of dozen times. Some of us liked to pamper our butts, but this paper was thick and coarse. Because of the thickness and quality of the paper, there was even less than it appeared, so each roll didn't go nearly as far as we were used to, a critical problem with so many men using so few rolls. Something had to be done about this situation.

As mentioned, some instructors at the academy had family members who sent them care packages from home. Some of these would be filled with toilet rolls, so these lucky few would bring their own rolls with them when they went to use the toilet, and take them away when they left. By noon each day, the nine rolls left by the Iraqi janitors would be long gone, leaving nothing for any evening visits to the toilet.

The search for a roll of toilet paper was therefore a constant battle. People would often grab one of the rolls and hang onto it, bringing it with them to and from the toilet, which often left others to do without. While all of us endured hardships and did our best to work together and share things, when it came to toilet paper it was every man for himself. Life in the Tin Hut definitely had its challenges.

On one end of the main hallway of the hut, there was a small table which held the boxes for our cable TV and internet service. We were able to receive several channels of Armed Forces Television on the small TVs provided in each of our rooms. Each room also had two internet connections as well with Ethernet cables. This alone made life a little bit more bearable—being able to surf the net and stay in touch with loved ones was important to all of us.

Of course, the internet didn't always work, but it was fairly reliable. We had to take precautions, though, by covering the components on the small table with plastic trash bags, as the Iraqi janitors didn't mind where they threw their buckets of water when mopping the floor. If the electronics had been shorted out there would be no telling how long it might take to get replacements—we would be without television and the means to contact loved ones back home if that had happened.

On one occasion, one of the instructors from the Blue Lagoon was seen leaving the Tin Hut with our internet router concealed beneath his clothes. Apparently, the router that covered the Blue Lagoon barracks wasn't as reliable as ours, so he'd decided to just take it upon himself to make a switch, taking ours and leaving their router in its place.

On the exterior of the shower rooms, on each side of the Tin Hut but contained within the high concrete blast walls, were two large water tanks, each holding probably a thousand gallons of water. One of these tanks was there to collect waste water and the other held potable water for use in the showers. The tanks had to be filled and emptied on a regular basis by trucks inspected and cleared to enter the compound. I always worried that the waste water tank would take a direct hit from a mortar round and spray crap all over the compound, and anyone walking, standing, or sitting around the campfire outside would have been covered in it. It was a common joke among us that we would be right next to one of the 'shit trucks' when it took a direct hit from a mortar, and we would end up dying covered in the stuff. Someone would have to be called in to identify our bodies and their first response would be, "I never liked him, he was a piece of shit anyway."

The Tin Hut sat in the middle of a fairly large parking area, with numerous military Humvees and other tactical vehicles parked all around in neat rows. As already mentioned, the Tin Hut was surrounded by very high concrete blast walls, maybe 15 or 20 feet tall, so the 'scenery' outside the window of your room was pretty much limited to a view of concrete. Made out of flimsy metal, the hut needed these walls around it to afford some protection. Without them, even a near miss by a mortar round would have destroyed it. Of course, a direct hit by a round coming from above would still have been the end of the hut, and everyone inside of it.

One evening, while I was inside my room, I suddenly heard a loud yelp from across the hallway. Wallie had been sitting in his room with his legs crossed on his lower bunk, watching television. An AK-47 round had pierced the ceiling of the Tin Hut and lodged itself in the calf of his leg. Somewhere in Baghdad, an Iraqi had fired his weapon into the air and, as the old saying goes, 'What goes up must come down'. Whether it was 'happy fire' or something more serious, we couldn't know. Either way, Wallie ended up with a unique souvenir.

He let out a loud wail, which got an immediate response from me. As I entered his room, I saw him looking down and pointing at this bullet sticking out of his lower leg. He then reached down and plucked it out. There was a small amount of blood, as it had actually pierced his flesh, along with the small depression made by the round as it impacted his leg. He wasn't seriously injured but within a few days a nasty infection set in, which gave him some problems for quite a while. That was the second time Wallie had been 'wounded'. He was able to keep the bullet and I suggested he have a hole drilled through it so he could wear it on a chain around his neck as a good luck charm. Oftentimes, as we walked across the compound, we would find spent rounds on the ground, but this was the first one that came down from above and actually hit one of us.

One way we dealt with the monotony of living and working at the academy was to try to find diversions or create a little fun. Before long, many of the doors to the rooms inside the Tin Hut were decorated with 'sandbag art', which I was responsible for thanks to my minor talent as an artist. Jimmy Two Dogs and Baghdad Boob wanted a sandbag hanging on the outside of their door with 'Mortar-Ritaville' drawn on it, so I went to work. They thought the name was perfect since mortars were dropped into our compound fairly often, and it did seem rather fitting.

I used a black marker pen and drew some palm trees amid explosions, and included Jimmy's and Bob's monikers as well. It became a hit and the next thing I knew, I was doing the same thing for other occupants. This kind of got carried to the extreme later on, once we moved into the new barracks and had individual rooms. Jimmy asked me to do one for him that depicted two dogs having sex 'doggy style', which went along with his nickname. It usually only took me a few minutes to conceive an idea and then draw it onto the sandbag.

Ted and I then put one on our door, and I soon had orders for sandbag art that kept me busy for at least a day or two. We always did what we could to make the rooms feel a little more like home, to brighten things up. Since the Tin Hut was going to be our home for quite a while, we tried to add our own little touches to bring some 'class' to the place. It was maybe not particularly wise from an OPSEC standpoint, but since I was only using nicknames, and not real names, I didn't think it mattered too much.

CHAPTER 10

Choir Practice

Some of us had purchased folding lawn chairs from the small PX on FOB Shield, or had bought ones at the big PX in the Green Zone. Our first evening after arriving at the academy was the first of many where we would sit around outside the Tin Hut and regale each other with our stories of the days' events, or share 'war stories' and anecdotes from our careers. It usually made for an entertaining evening and allowed us to let off some steam. Naturally, we could count on the input from Jimmy Two Dogs to keep us in stitches. He always had a funny story to share. The evening gatherings outside the Tin Hut became a nightly ritual that would be expanded upon during our stay.

With some free time on my hands until classes actually started, I was out exploring one day and noticed a nearby army unit had built a fire pit outside their barracks by digging a hole in the ground. This looked like a good idea, having a fire to sit around each evening. People always enjoy sitting around a fire, plus it would help to take the chill off the cool nights in Baghdad at that time of year.

Unfortunately, the Tin Hut sat right on top of a hard paved surface, so digging a hole to create a pit was out of the question. While walking around the compound, however, I noticed a pile of discarded bricks, stacked outside one of the nearby vacant buildings. Since it didn't appear that they were being used for anything, I started gathering them up several at a time and taking them back to the Tin Hut. I built a small rectangular 'fire box', about six bricks deep on all sides. It measured about one yard square in size. This would become our 'bonding' place from that point on, and even though it wasn't really a pit, that's what we called it.

That first evening, when people started gathering around outside the Tin Hut to chat before going to the chow hall, I had already started a small fire inside the pit, using scraps of wood scrounged from around the compound. After that first night, the fires became such a ritual that we began to have other visitors stop by to join in with our evening gatherings. Some of them were welcome, others not so much.

Our fire pit went through a couple of different designs, depending on the materials at hand. The original bricks eventually disintegrated from the heat of the nightly fires, and the pit finally morphed into what can only be described as a 'Texas Bar-B-Que pit' without legs—one half of a 55-gallon drum, provided by one of the KBR employees working at Camp Shield who took pity on us. It actually worked out really well. It didn't deteriorate from the heat like the bricks did.

Finding wood to burn was another issue. We started off using discarded wooden crates and boxes. We had to scavenge around the academy grounds, since it wasn't in abundance, so each evening some of us would go around the compound looking for scraps. Eventually, one of the KBR workers assigned to Camp Shield came by in a front-loader tractor and dropped a ton of tree limbs for us to use. Small trees and shrubs had been cut down to clear ground for some new buildings, and they had saved the wood for us. It was as though we had hit the mother lode—no more frantic searches for wood for our nightly fire. It got downright cool in the evenings, even cold sometimes, so the fire made it possible for us to sit around outside visiting with each other. And sitting with company outside was preferable to just sitting inside our small rooms in the Tin Hut.

When people think about Baghdad, they think about the oppressive heat, which is indeed an accurate depiction of conditions in summer. During the day time it can reach 130 degrees in the middle of the summer, but in the wintertime it is very pleasant during the day, mostly in the 70s and 80s. It can also get chilly at night out of doors during the winter months. And it's a fact that men like playing with fire. Once the fire pit was up and burning for the night, every guy had to take his turn poking at the fire, moving the wood around and generally just doing what guys do when they're around a fire, which is mess with it. Usually we would get the fire going once evening chow was over. Whoever was first back at the Tin Hut would take charge of getting it started for the evening's gathering.

Combustibles to get the fire started were another problem until Jimmy Two Dogs solved that issue. Bits of paper, cardboard, dried scrub brush, anything that we could use to get the fire going, was often difficult to find. Since Camp Shield was a U.S. military facility, it was kept pretty clean, and there wasn't always trash lying around that we could use. Jimmy found a solution by taking a small coffee can he had found and then squirming beneath one of the Humvees parked nearby and stealing some diesel fuel from it. (This would become the basis for one of the practical jokes we played, which involved Jimmy Two Dogs and a friend of his who was a new arrival to the Baghdad Police Academy). Jimmy would show up to the fire pit with his little coffee can full of fuel, pour the contents onto the wood inside the fire pit, and whoosh, we had fire.

The fact that we could purchase alcohol made the fire pit our own little 'bar area' after we settled into life at the Academy. It was common for these nightly gatherings to start up after classes and before evening chow, break up during the dinner hour, and then recommence with a fire following dinner. Most people would sit outside for an hour or two and then drift away, going back into their room or maybe visiting the army's MWR facility. A few die-hards would sometimes stay later into the night, especially on Thursdays, which started the Iraqi weekend. There were no classes for the next two days.

Sometimes the evening discussions would last until well after midnight. Other times they would end at a reasonable hour and everyone would retire to their room in the 'hootch'. You could usually count on Jimmy Two Dogs and Baghdad Boob being present around the fire pit for a while each evening. Others would come and go, more or less filtering in and out as the evening progressed. Occasionally the academy director, Malcolm, would stop by briefly and chat with us for a few minutes, though we could never understand a word because his Scottish accent was so heavy. He would talk to us for five or 10 minutes and after he left we would all look at each other and in unison ask, "Did anybody understand a word he said?" Then we'd all laugh. Cutting up and self-deprecating humor was par for the course, as well as needling and poking fun at others. For the most part it was all good natured, though some people, like Halleluiah Mack, came in for some brutal treatment.

We were always on the lookout for ways to make a more comfortable and congenial environment. While passing by one of the FOB buildings one day, which contained a little vendor area run by a local Iraqi, I noticed a sofa-like piece of outdoor furniture, more or less like a piece of wicker patio furniture. It seated two people and it came with a matching chair. This looked perfect for us so I negotiated a price with the Iraqi and snatched it up. Once I got it back to the 'hootch' and set it by the fire pit, it added an almost 'living room' atmosphere for our little nightly gatherings. It became our own little patio, complete with patio furniture.

It wasn't unusual for people to donate other items for the cause. With the money we were making, people could easily afford to purchase items from the Iraqis frequenting the FOB. And yes, making so much more money than most of us were accustomed to could cause you to become a bit careless. I guess you could also say that the fire pit served as another diversion from the day-in, day-out monotony for us. Looking for ways to improve our social gathering place helped to relieve the boredom. We were always on the look-out for things to provide a little entertainment and a break from the daily drudgery.

Which brings me to the nicknames some of us were given. One evening, while a group of us were camped out around the fire pit, someone told the joke about the young Native American boy who asks his father how he got his name. His father answers, "When your sister was born I stepped out of the teepee and the first thing I saw was a morning dove, so I named her 'Morning Dove'. And your brother, when he was born the first thing I saw was a soaring eagle, so I named him 'Soaring Eagle'. Why do you ask, 'Two Dogs Fucking'?" The joke brought down the house and got some huge belly laughs from everyone present, especially Jimmy.

A few days later, several of us were headed to the chow hall for lunch, including Jimmy. We needed to drop our clothes off at the laundry on the way. Outside the laundry sat a young Iraqi man with a very ancient sewing machine. For a few dollars, he'd sew your name in Arabic lettering on your shirts just above the pocket. Some had it sewn onto their 'booney hats' as well, kind of like a nametag. Jimmy decided to pay the Iraqi man to have this done for all of his shirts.

After Jimmy walked away from Bob and me, we got a great idea. Since Jimmy loved the joke that had been told a few evenings earlier, we bargained with the Iraqi to have him sew a different name onto Jimmy's shirts. At first he was hesitant, but when we started peeling off dollar bills we were able to convince him to go along with our scheme. Unbeknownst to Jimmy, when he picked his shirts up a couple of days later, the stitching in Arabic on his shirt was not his name, but instead read 'Two Dogs Fucking' in Arabic.

Proudly, Jimmy wore his shirt to his next class the following morning. His poor Iraqi cadets, out of deference and politeness, did not ask him about what was written on his shirt for half the day. Finally, during the lunch break, his translator asked him, "Mr. Jim, why do you say this on your shirt?" Jimmy looked at him somewhat quizzically and said, "It's my name, 'Jimmy', why do you ask?" The translator then told him what the writing actually said. Throughout the compound you could hear Jimmy bellowing, "You motherfuckers!" From that day forth, Jimmy was affectionately referred to as 'Two Dogs', or 'Jimmy Two Dogs', a name that would stick with him throughout our time together at the Baghdad Police Academy.

Jimmy's roommate, Bob, was eventually given the nickname of 'Baghdad Boob' which had nothing to do with the fact that he had been an IRS Special Agent in an earlier life. Bob's name was derived as a result of a typo on the part of the same Iraqi with the sewing machine. Or I guess you could call it a 'stitch-o'. Bob had asked him to sew 'Baghdad Bob' on his shirts, but instead he ended up with 'Baghdad Boob'. My roommate, Ted, had asked the man to sew his name on his shirts, both in Arabic and English. Hence his name, 'Ted Both', being sewn in Arabic when he picked his shirts up from the laundry. Though not stitched on my shirts (maybe I was gun-shy, or perhaps 'sewing machine-shy'), I was given the nickname 'R-Del', an invention of Jimmy's. To this day

I don't really know where that came from or what it meant. I may not want to know.

Halleluiah Mack was not a fan of, nor did he like us using, nicknames. He also didn't like the sandbag art on the doors of our rooms in the Tin Hut. He especially didn't like us using our nicknames when communicating with each other on our walkie-talkies. And he especially didn't like our nightly choir practices. It was all unprofessional in his mind, I'm sure. We didn't really care, it was just Halleluiah Mack.

Mack walked by our fire pit, or more accurately patrolled by, every evening to see what kind of debauchery we were up to. After he walked by, and when he thought he was out of our view, he would pull his small notebook from his shirt pocket and start to jot down notes. I'm not sure what he ever did with his little notebook, but it made for a lot of fun for us around the fire pit. We would laugh and joke about its contents, to the merriment of all. Oftentimes our derision likely carried over to Mack as he was walking away, but we didn't care whether he heard us or not. The guy was an idiot. At least that was the consensus of everyone in our group. I'm sure his little notes were shared with the leadership back in the Green Zone, telling them we were all a bunch of drunks and an embarrassment to the ICITAP program, which was far from the truth. Okay, maybe using nicknames on the radio was a deviation from norms, but since we were never given any written rules or protocols to follow, it's hard to really criticize us for that.

Another situation that led to some consternation on the part of Halleluiah Mack was when the 1st Cavalry Division moved out of Camp Shield. When they departed from their half of the base, they left behind a great deal of 'creature comforts'. At least they were creature comforts considering the austere conditions we were living in. Since the Iraqi military was going to move into the area vacated by the 1st Cav, I told everyone to go over and grab what they could before the Iraqis laid claim to it.

It became basically a large-scale scrounging operation. Academy instructors, especially the newest arrivals, who had very little, went back and forth, liberating as many items as they could carry. That is until Halleluiah Mack happened to see what was going on. Mack objected

CHOIR PRACTICE • 101

loudly, saying that we were "stealing from the Iraqis"—the same Iraqis he had denigrated and insulted during his earlier academy orientation presentation. All of a sudden he had developed a concern for the poor men who would be moving into the former 1st Cav area.

Needless to say, his sudden concern for Iraqis over his fellow American cops didn't endear him to us. Mack went running to the military police unit that was still assigned to the academy and complained to their first sergeant. He then went to the academy director and argued that we should stop our thievery and return everything that we had taken. When word got back to us that we needed to return all the pilfered items, none of us returned a thing, though we did have to scale back our trips over to the Iraqi side of the compound, or at least be more discreet when stealing everything that wasn't nailed down. Personally, I got away with a very nice large pedestal fan, which we used to try and dry things up in the main hallway of the Tin Hut.

Another diversion we engaged in was high-stakes poker games. It wasn't hard to find one taking place somewhere on the compound on any given evening. Most were interesting affairs, right out of the Old West—a bunch of men sitting around a poker table, all wearing side-arms or shoulder holsters, with a pile of money and poker chips on the table. It was an interesting sight to see. The very first game I joined was an eye-opening experience. Large pots of money transferred back and forth across the table and plenty of alcohol was involved, but nobody ever got shot.

Over the years, I had played many games of 'nickel, dime, quarter' poker, where the average winning pot might be a dollar or two, but these pots would sometimes reach a couple of hundred dollars or more. When the dealer started calling, 'deuces, one-eyed jacks, black sevens, and whatever card followed a queen' as wild cards, I decided it was time for me to leave the table. It would take 10 aces to win a poker hand. During one game I lost about $400 in three minutes! I hadn't come to Iraq to gamble away all the money that I was making.

Most nights, though, we just sat around the camp fire. One day we hit another jackpot, when an old building was torn down and we scavenged a lot of the wood from it, which gave us enough to last for several years.

We stacked it up neatly outside the Tin Hut, but behind the blast walls to hide it, so that no one would come by and steal it.

It's hard to describe, because most people will never understand unless they too lived in a war zone, or had developed that 'gallows humor' that most cops have, but our evenings around the fire pit are something I will remember forever. It's what helped us all keep our sanity during some very tough and lonely times away from loved ones. It also helped bring us together and bind us together forever as brothers in arms. It was a great group of people leaning on each other for support under difficult circumstances, and giving support back when one of the others needed it.

Gentlemen, Start Your Engines

It was an interesting experience to say the least when we arrived at the large gymnasium as our first classes were getting ready to start. Utter chaos would be the appropriate description, I think, with Halleluiah Mack leading the way. The gym was filled with about a thousand prospective Iraqi police cadets, seated in and milling around the bleachers on one side of the structure.

My colleagues and I stood back and watched Halleluiah Mack running around shouting at people, giving directions, and accomplishing absolutely nothing. The cadets just looked at him like he was a crazy man. Apparently, little or no thought had gone into how to actually process all these new cadets, get them assigned to a class, and then make arrangements for billeting all of them. The steady din of conversation among them became almost a roar as they started to get restless because of how fouled-up things were.

Some of them would be told to move over to another location in the gym, only to be directed back to where they had come from a few minutes later. The confusion was starting to piss off not only the Iraqis, but also us instructors. There seemed to be no rhyme nor reason for some of the instructions being barked out.

I never really figured out how my class actually got assigned to me, as there seemed to be no real process as to how the cadets were divided up. If there was, it was never shared with us instructors—we had been kept in the dark as to how this was all being set up. Sometime during the preceding days, I had been assigned a partner instructor, Kenny, the former DeKalb County, Georgia, police officer who had come over to Iraq with Stan and Ruby. Kenny was a good guy and we got along well. Kenny was also the guy who had fallen out of his bunk and landed on his head that night back in the Adnan Palace. He appeared no worse for wear though, maybe just an inch or two shorter. He was the perfect, more relaxed counter to my highly strung personality. Kenny was laid back and quiet, whereas I had a tendency to be more vocal and animated, especially about what I perceived as lies and bullshit, which we had encountered extreme amounts of from the day we arrived in Lorton, Virginia. Admittedly, it's always been a shortcoming of mine, not being able to bite my tongue.

Once we eventually found out who our cadets were, Kenny and I worked to separate them from all the rest, who were still milling around or being shuffled into different groups. Once we were officially given our release from this major clusterfuck, the huge throng of Iraqi cadets started moving towards their billeting area. Fortunately, Kenny and I had been able to position our cadets towards the front of this mass of people, and we struggled mightily to keep our group together as we walked towards the rows of barracks. We didn't want to go through another clusterfuck trying to find them all again once we'd reached our destination.

The billeting consisted of prefabricated, rectangular, one-story barracks buildings with four entrance doors, two on each end. Each barracks contained about 25 sets of bunk beds. There were no wall lockers or any other creature comforts—spartan accommodation to say the very least. There were no assigned barracks, so it was basically a free-for-all—first come, first served, so to speak. As an instructor, you laid claim to a building as quickly as you could, then you stationed a couple of cadets at each entrance to stop people from other classes getting in. This alone was a battle, because other cadets kept trying to peek inside to see if our barracks were better than theirs. We really wanted to keep our class together and separate from all the others to help control them better and so as not to lose track any of them.

Kenny and I quickly staked out the first building we came to, which would accommodate our class of approximately 25 cadets. We got them inside the barracks with the help of a translator. There was also a secondary motive for keeping our class together, and that was to hopefully instill some *esprit de corps* and get them thinking of themselves as a team. A little good-natured competition can be a positive motivator, especially in this kind of environment. We felt that the more they lived and worked together, the better they would perform in the classroom, and hopefully on the streets of Iraq as police officers once they graduated.

Fortunately, the barracks we selected had bunk beds that had already been assembled, including mattresses, though some of them were rather rickety. Other barracks contained large piles of unassembled bunk bed parts, that had just been dropped in the middle of the floor—a rather difficult proposition when there were no tools provided. Plus, by this time it was getting late and it would be dark pretty soon, and since there was also no electricity in the barracks for some reason, assembling the beds after dark was going to be a real challenge.

Most of us instructors carried small multi-tools in a case on our belts, but they certainly weren't ideal for putting together a bunk bed. They consisted of several different blades and screw driver heads, and something resembling a pair of pliers. Kenny and I had been lucky, although even our bunk beds hadn't been put together too well. They were wobbly to say the least—the screws and nuts and bolts had not been properly tightened, more 'thumb-screwed' into place. I gave my multi-tool to one of the cadets and instructed him to tighten up all the beds and to protect my tool with his life. He was instructed not to loan it to any cadets from other classes as I would never see it again if that happened. It was his responsibility to make sure I got it back, and I could see fear in his eyes. He was warned what would happen to him if my tool disappeared, but there was really nothing I could have done. It was a warning without teeth, but he didn't know that.

Once we had our barracks, word came down from the academy leadership that we should take our class to another location on the campus, where they could draw some bedding. By this time it was getting close to the end of the work day for the academy's Iraqi staff. In order to preserve our place in the barracks and not lose anything, we selected several cadets to stay behind and guard against anyone coming in and taking over our barracks, or absconding with the assembled bunk beds.

We then led the rest of our cadets to draw bedding at a cluster of admin buildings, perhaps a hundred yards away, promising to take care of those left behind. Moving our cadets to the linen office proved to be something of a challenge, but we were able to get everyone there and they were each issued a couple of sheets. They were much too small for the mattresses, but the cadets would have to make do with what was issued. They were also each given a light blanket to cover up with—the barracks had no heating.

Once that was completed, we returned to the barracks, only to be met with a stream of complaints (in Arabic) from our cadets about not having any pillows. Once we figured out what they were complaining about, and instead of just sitting there bitching and whining as some of the instructors were doing, I grabbed three 'volunteers' and told them to follow me. Kenny stayed with the rest of the cadets inside the barracks.

With my volunteers, I returned to the linen office, but I was told that the place to draw pillows was closed for the day. I couldn't believe it. Here we had a thousand cadets trying to get settled into the academy for the night, and the offices that were intended to provide support were closed or closing. It was the end of their day (though ours was far from over), and they were headed back to the comfort of their home and their families, literally abandoning the new cadets. It had been a long day for all of us, but this was flat-out unacceptable to me. Plus, I didn't want a riot on my hands from a bunch of unhappy cadets who couldn't sleep without a pillow. I asked for and was given the name of the person in charge and, with my cadet volunteers in tow, I was able to track him down in an adjacent courtyard. Once I had him cornered I demanded that he open up the room so I could draw some pillows for my class. He refused, advising me that his office was closed and that I would have to come back the next day and sign for the pillows, so that he wouldn't be held accountable.

It was obvious I wasn't going to get anywhere with him, so I thanked him for his help and we all walked the short distance to the building where the pillows were stored. Once he was out of sight, my cadets and I kicked the door in. It only took one good kick and the wood around the lock shattered. We scrounged around and found a huge net-like piece of material in an adjacent room. The net was made out of some kind of strong cording, and we stuffed 25 pillows into it—it was actually pretty heavy once we finished loading it up. We then quickly departed the area, hoping that no one had seen us. If they did they never reported us, since I was never called on the carpet for 'breaking and entering'.

We made it back with our load of pillows and a sense of accomplishment and relief settled in. We had gotten our cadets billeted, provided them with sheets, blankets, and now pillows, and had bedded them down for the night. Compared to some of our fellow instructors, our day had gone pretty smoothly, and I only had to commit one burglary to accomplish our mission. No shots were fired, and nobody got assaulted. We would later hear that some of our other instructors didn't fare as well, and as best as I can determine I still owe the government for 25 pillows, as I don't think they were ever turned back in. Once our class graduated, I believe the pillows left with them when they departed the academy.

That evening, around our camp fire, we were told by a passer-by that Carly had had a pretty rough day. At one point she had become distraught and upset over how things were going, and the fact that her cadets had become vocal over her inability to solve any problems. Apparently, they started shouting in Arabic and demanding help, upon which she panicked and drew her weapon on them, threatening to shoot them all. It seems that instead of just sucking it up and finding a solution to a problem, Carly was one of those who just stammered, shuffled around, and eventually became unable to cope—and her cadets fed off her panicking and her inability to take care of their needs, which just made a bad situation that much worse. Carly obviously wasn't suited for this kind of work or environment.

I didn't witness this incident myself, but having heard the story from a number of people who did witness it, I could only conclude that there must have been some truth to it. In fact, I was told that Carly had 'lost it' and was near a nervous breakdown because she couldn't handle the pressure. This was something you might expect from someone who had never served as a police officer before and was placed in such a stressful situation, in a difficult atmosphere. It was not fair to her, really, and whoever made the decision to involve her in the program deserves criticism. Carly was way out of her element.

The next day we met our cadets early at their barracks and rounded them up to escort them to the Iraqi chow hall for breakfast, where we left them until they were finished. We then gathered them back together outside their barracks, and told them that today they would be issued police informs.

As a group, we instructors were concerned about issuing real Iraqi Police (IP) uniforms to the cadets. It was common knowledge that these uniforms often found their way into the hands of the insurgency and were used to commit acts of terror in and around Baghdad. As most of us had experienced during our careers back in America, when we attended our own police academies, we suggested the cadets be issued something like khakis to wear instead of actual IP uniforms. Naturally our suggestions were met with the standard refrain of 'window or aisle'. No one in the Green Zone wanted to hear it. When we pushed the issue, we were told that the reason Iraqi cadets were issued actual IP uniforms was to instill a sense of camaraderie and belonging to them. It was total bullshit, but I guess it was the best answer they could come up with. My guess is that no one ever really put any thought into it, or realized that issuing real uniforms to the cadets might not be a good idea. As had happened before, once they had their uniforms in hand some cadets never showed up again, simply disappearing into the fabric of Baghdad society. Likely the insurgency ended up with brand new sets of uniforms to help them carry out terrorist attacks.

Once we got the IP uniforms issued to our cadets, we informed them that they were released for the rest of the day. There were no classes yet, nor any other admin-related chores that could be accomplished. Kenny and I followed our class back to their barracks and checked to make sure that they had no issues. It was a short day for us and it was soon time to head back to the Tin Hut.

Training wouldn't actually start for a couple more days, so as an organization we had some time to regroup and hopefully do a better job with our cadets come day one of classes. They deserved better from instructors who were making so much money. They deserved better treatment and good-quality training. Plus, it was a matter of pride for many of us. The Iraqis had been told that we were the experts in law enforcement, and in our first test some of us had failed miserably. Our lack of preparation was embarrassing. Not only the Iraqis were watching us but the U.S. military was watching as well. Much of the military saw us as a bunch of over-paid prima donnas and that first day some of us certainly proved them correct. The fiasco at the gym the day before was a huge embarrassment, followed by the billeting challenges and mistakes. Many of us certainly had not shone. Kenny and I believed we had done well and had made a good initial impression on our cadets, but it was going to be a long six weeks, with plenty of opportunities for us to stumble. We would need to stay on top of our game.

The cadets really deserved a better training program. The basic course was only six weeks long. Plus, being taught through a translator presented its own problems and slowed the process down to a crawl. It was not nearly enough time to turn them into good cops by Iraqi standards, and definitely not by American standards.

Realistically, in most major metropolitan areas of America, a basic police academy program lasts six months or more just for the basic training, followed by a period of field training, along with regular in-service training sessions throughout an officer's career. In my case, the basic course was 660 hours at the St. Louis Police Academy. Since then it's been raised to 900 hours. This would be followed by up to 12 weeks of riding along with an experienced officer before you were cut loose to work alone. And then you had a probationary period of one year, during which time an officer's employment could be terminated for pretty much any reason, but especially if you screwed up or just didn't perform well enough to instill your supervisors with confidence that you were capable of doing the job without getting yourself or anyone else killed.

Iraqi cadets were taught basic patrol techniques, much like we would teach cadets in an American academy—what to look for while on patrol, how to conduct a traffic stop, how to use position to your advantage—as well as trying to help them develop observation skills and things of that nature. I'm not sure how much value there was in this, as Iraqi police didn't really 'patrol' neighborhoods in the way that American cops do.

American cops also try to be proactive and are out looking for problems, whereas in Iraq people came to the police station and reported them. The IPs might respond, or they might not. They might write a report if so inclined, or they might just tell the person to come back the next day. Some of it came down to one's family or tribal name, or even one's religion. Shia versus Sunni was still a bone of contention among Iraqis, with the poor Iraqi Christians and other minority religions basically left out in the cold.

Obviously the cadets received instruction in Iraqi statutes and laws, so that they had an understanding of what was illegal, though they might not actually enforce any laws or make any arrests. New laws and rules were being put into place following the fall of Saddam, and this portion of the training was taught by an Iraqi lawyer.

They also received instruction in what is commonly referred to in the U.S. as 'defensive tactics'. This basically consists of how to protect and defend oneself without using a firearm, using non-lethal tactics and weapons instead. This included training in what was referred to as the 'use of force continuum'—mere presence, verbal commands, soft hand, more forceful physical intervention, non-lethal weapons (pepper spray, mace, batons), and finally use of deadly force. Plastic police batons or nightsticks were provided, so the students could whack the hell out of each other while learning how to effectively use a real baton. They were taught takedown moves and pressure-point techniques—many of the same things being taught to American police cadets in academies back in the U.S.

A one-hour block of instruction was set aside for marching—basically drill and ceremony practice. Cadets would go out to the parade ground and march around for an hour. It was actually rather humorous watching them do the Iraqi 'foot stomp' march. They would take three steps and then stomp the ground with their right foot (my guess is this was a carry-over from the Saddam days). It was actually one of the few things the cadets did really well. They were good little marchers.

Firearms training was also a large part of the course and time had to be set aside at the academy range for them to shoot both a 9mm pistol and an AK-47 automatic rifle. Since one never knew where the cadets' loyalties truly lay, whether with the new government or the insurgency, I was never comfortable giving them a loaded weapon and standing around the range with them. Kudos to the American instructors who did that.

Actual training amounted to no more than four hours of instruction per day. When one considers that each class (excepting the Iraqi law class, which was taught in Arabic by an Iraqi lawyer), as well as the marching, was taught through a translator, things moved slowly. Some cadets spoke good English, but all questions and answers had to be translated so that every student in class could benefit from the exchange. It really limited how much could be accomplished in a six-week course.

They deserved better from us, but the priority for the U.S. and Iraqi governments was getting as many police out onto the streets of Baghdad as quickly as possible. Since we had disbanded the entire Iraqi police force following the invasion, police protection or even police presence was pretty much non-existent. 'Cannon fodder' was n term that fit the cadets pretty well, at least that was our impression of what as being accomplished with a six-week program taught through translators. 'Window or aisle' was the standard answer to our suggestions for a longer course length.

CHAPTER 12

Iraqi Chow

When the 1st Cav departed the FOB it was a sad day indeed—we had gotten used to eating quite well at their chow hall. As mentioned, arrangements had been made ahead of time to provide food for us until a new army unit came in and set up a new chow hall. This was expected to take a couple of weeks, and in the meantime we had to eat from an Iraqi-catered buffet line set up in the AA Building. This was an interesting experience to say the least.

I recall the very first time I walked the buffet line and saw what appeared to be several different types of meat dishes. I asked the server, "What's that?" and he responded, "Chicken," in a very enthusiastic voice. As I continued down the line and pointed at the different meats, I got the same response every time. "Chicken." I surmised that 'chicken' was the only word of English the server knew, and I'm not sure to this day what I was eating. I'm inclined to think that pigeon was more likely. I can't recall ever seeing a chicken the whole time I was in Iraq, and kind of like the Chinese restaurant joke, I don't recall seeing many pigeons around Camp Shield. But I never woke up in the middle of the night with the need to make a mad rush to the toilet, so I guess the food was okay. No one else ever complained about any adverse reactions either, and to be truthful the Iraqi catering company did a pretty fair job of providing us with decent meals. It was a relief for all of us, though, when we finally got a new army chow hall set up, and it turned out to be just as good as the previous one. Once again, the U.S. military knows how to put on a spread of food.

CHAPTER 13

Happy New Year!

New Year's Eve at the Baghdad Police Academy was an unexpected surprise for us all. Arrangements had been made to bring in a buffet and a boatload of liquor. There was all kinds of food and munchies available, lots of snacks as well as platters of meat. It was a veritable feast. The beverage selection was also pretty awesome—just about every kind of booze, beer, and wine you could ask for. The food and drink had been delivered via a PSD coming over from the Green Zone. If the insurgents had ambushed that convoy it would have been a tragedy. We held a party inside one of the new barracks, which had recently been occupied by the group that had preceded us in the Tin Hut. There was a lot of conversation, a great deal of laughter, and a bit of drinking on the part of all in attendance, which was pretty much every Westerner at the academy.

One of the attendees had a traditional Iraqi headdress, which we all passed around so we could get our photograph taken wearing it. Lots of jokes and police war stories were told and some minor pranks were pulled. All in all it was a really good party, not what we expected being in the middle of a war zone in a Muslim country, but the merriment ended eventually and we all stumbled back to our rooms.

It's a damn good thing there was no insurgent attack that night, because we'd never have been able to shoot straight to defend ourselves. At midnight Baghdad time, the city exploded with small-arms fire as Iraqis stepped outside of their homes and fired off their guns to ring in the new year. Omaha Beach must have sounded like this on D-Day.

One benefit of getting drunk together was the way it allowed us to get better acquainted, at least for one night, with the other groups at the academy. For one evening anyway, we all came together. Unfortunately, it didn't last beyond New Year's Eve and the next day everyone was back in their own little cliques.

CHAPTER 14

Roll Call and Bomb Drills

The first day of classes proved to be a memorable one, partly as a result of the managed chaos going on around us, and partly because of the 'safety drill' conducted by my co-instructor and me. The instruction area was some distance from the Tin Hut. It was a good five minutes' walk to get to the classrooms, which consisted of row after row of thin metal buildings, a little smaller than the Tin Hut. Outside the classrooms there were concrete bunkers, like the ones at the Adnan Palace and all over the Green Zone, where you could seek temporary protection during a rocket or mortar attack. A direct hit on a classroom would have killed everyone inside, and likely most of those in the classrooms on either side as well.

After our group of cadets had filed into our assigned classroom, Kenny and I asked our translator, Ahmed, to have the students write their names on slips of paper and place them on their desks to be translated into English. It was amazing how many students in one class were named 'Mohammed'. It made for an interesting daily roll call to say the least. You called out "Mohammed?" and most of the hands in the class were raised and the cadets shouted out, "Here! Here! Here!" in Arabic. You get the point.

We then gave the class an introduction and details of our experience in law enforcement. Kenny talked about his experience in Georgia and I mentioned mine in the St. Louis area. Both Kenny and I had worked a variety of jobs in our careers, and the students seemed to be impressed that in America you could actually progress in your career based on merit and hard work, and not on your family name or tribal affiliation.

The cadets sat there in what appeared to be rapt attention as Kenny and I described our careers. They truly seemed interested in these strange Americans who had come to teach them how to be cops.

Kenny and I viewed them as blank canvasses in a sense, since their impression of law enforcement was quite different to ours. In their world, the police held a position of power and prestige and held sway over society in general. Police under Saddam were certainly not 'service oriented'. Corruption and brutality were rampant and the people viewed them more as the enemy than people who were there to help them. Of course we couldn't say it was always different back in America, since there are some people there who also see the police as the enemy, though most have a much more favorable view.

We had to do our best to change that way of thinking among our cadets, and replace it with a genuine care and concern for their neighbors and their communities. It was a daunting task. They didn't have history and the U.S. Constitution to guide them, as American cops did. In a tribal environment like Iraq, getting the cadets to understand the importance of enforcing the law equally was a foreign concept, and after decades of brutal dictatorships, especially under Saddam and his two sons, it was going to be even harder to change their way of thinking. Under Saddam, to be a police officer was to gain power and control of your neighbors, and to receive payoffs. Corruption was simply rampant.

One of the first things we decided to do was to establish a safety drill for our students. Since the academy was a constant target for insurgent mortars or rockets, it seemed prudent to have some sort of evacuation drill for the class in the event of an attack. Just a couple of months earlier, the academy had been targeted for mortar attack for over 30 consecutive days, with varying numbers of rounds striking the compound. Fortunately, casualties were light during that month of attacks, with only a few cadets wounded and only one American instructor receiving a slight shrapnel injury to his leg, but it was still a serious and ongoing concern. Through our translator, Ahmed, we instructed the cadets that in the event of an attack they were to file out of the classroom quickly and take cover in one of the concrete bunkers outside.

ROLL CALL AND BOMB DRILLS • 119

The bunkers were able to accommodate maybe 15 people at most. As previously described, they were basically an upside down U-shaped concrete structure with an opening on each end. They were intended to provide some quick and temporary protection from incoming mortars, and were not designed for long-term stays. Mortar attacks were usually over quickly—the insurgents would fire off three, four or five rounds and then run for the hills, before any potential return fire from U.S. forces. As long as a mortar hit facing the sides of the bunker, you'd be fairly well protected, but if it landed outside one of the open ends, you'd definitely have a problem with shrapnel. A direct hit on a bunker probably would be have been fatal to most if not all occupants.

Kenny and I decided it would be a good idea to do a test run, to see how the cadets would react to a real emergency, so we decided to conduct a mortar attack drill. We instructed the cadets, through the translator, that if we shouted out "Bomb! Bomb! Bomb!", the cadets were to quickly but carefully file out of the room and get inside the closest bunker. It was reminiscent of fire drills held for elementary school children back in America for many years.

At the appointed moment, Kenny and I both shouted out the pre-arranged signal—"Bomb! Bomb! Bomb!"—and our cadets immediately got out of their seats and strode quickly towards the classroom door, exiting in single file. And so did all the rest of the cadets as well. Dozens of students spilled out of the classrooms and tried to cram into the bunkers.

In our fervor to train our cadets, we had forgotten that the classroom walls were paper thin and any loud noise in one classroom could be heard a couple of classrooms away. Unaware that we were practicing a mortar drill, all the other instructors assumed there was a true emergency situation and followed our lead, instructing their cadets to exit the classroom and take cover in the bunkers.

Needless to say, the managed chaos that had characterized the start of the day promptly returned, and all because of Kenny and me. It took quite a while to sort things out and get everyone back into their classrooms. Kenny and I, with very sheepish looks on our faces, approached the lead instructor and told him what had happened, that we were the culprits who had caused the classrooms to evacuate.

After the embarrassment and laughter died down, it was decided that it wasn't such a bad thing after all, since we'd now seen how the cadets reacted to a crisis (which really wasn't too bad), and it gave us a baseline to work on to improve the response in the event of a real mortar attack. But it did take a while for Kenny and me to live it down among our colleagues. For several days afterwards, when we walked passed a colleague on the way to the chow hall or the laundry we often heard in somewhat muffled voices (but loud enough for us to overhear), "Bomb, bomb, bomb."

Back in the classroom, after everything had calmed down, we went over the schedule for the cadets, laying out the course of instruction so they would know where we were taking them, as well as the goals that Kenny and I had established. The set curriculum was one thing, but Kenny and I also had our ideas of what our cadets would need to survive on the streets of Baghdad. We wanted to give them the very best preparation that we could.

We took our work seriously and did our best to impart to the cadets the things we had learned as cops back in America. We even tried to instill the *esprit de corps* that most police maintain, telling them that they should think of police work as a brotherhood. I doubt they really understood it the same way that cops in the U.S. do, but it was a start.

Noon finally arrived and the class was dismissed for lunch. The instructors headed towards the FOB and our own chow hall, while the cadets headed for the Iraqi chow hall, which wasn't far from the classroom area. I made the decision to sit and eat with my cadets, hoping to establish a bond between us. Little did I know that this small courtesy would establish me in their eyes as a true friend. I stood in line with them until our class was called inside. I maintained my place in line, ignoring offers for me to step forward ahead of my cadets. Once I got my tray filled with something that looked like chicken and some kind of beans, as well as some really good Iraqi bread, I proceeded to the table where my cadets were seated and joined them. So many of them were calling for me to sit next to them that I finally just had to grab the nearest seat and sit down. The Iraqi bread was the highlight of the meal. Fresh and warm, it was really good, but the rest of the meal wasn't anything to write home about.

There was so much chatter among my group of cadets, as well as looks and chatter from other tables in the chow hall, it would seem that I had done something previously unheard of—an American instructor actually spending time with and having lunch with his Iraqi cadets. There were looks of approval all around the hall. My snap decision had proven to be very popular, and I had made some friends among the students. I looked around the room and realized that I was the only American instructor eating with the cadets, a fact that wasn't lost on them. I had certainly set a precedent, and after that day other instructors would start to join their cadets for lunch. I would repeat this often with my class over the next few months.

Sadly, a year or so later this same hall would be attacked by dual suicide bombers, who killed over 40 cadets when they exploded their suicide vests both inside and right outside the building. No Americans were hurt, but in addition to those cadets killed there were many more injured, some seriously.

After finishing our first day of classes, we all returned to the Tin Hut to kill some time until dinner. Stories were exchanged and humorous anecdotes told over and over again about our first day with these new, raw cadets. And I got some questions about why I had made the decision to sit down and have lunch with my own students.

CHAPTER 15

How Much for the Woman?

One day, a PSD rolled into the academy to drop off a new instructor, sent over from the Adnan Palace. When Becky stepped out of the SUV those of us sitting around the fire pit immediately took notice. Becky was a very attractive and very well-built young lady in her mid to late twenties. That alone, in a compound where we had not seen many females at all, much less attractive ones, was enough to get our attention, but Becky also wore a small diamond stud on her nose and carried herself in a way that exuded confidence. Our first impression, from a distance, was that she looked like she had her shit together. We would soon learn that she did indeed.

Needless to say, the three of us sitting around the fire pit leapt to our feet and headed over to welcome the new addition to the Baghdad Police Academy. We even sucked in our guts as we approached the new arrival, though none of us were able to hold that for very long. That's why you have to keep moving around, it helps cover up your stomach hanging over your beltline a little bit.

Once introductions had been made, we escorted Becky over to the Tin Hut, where she would be staying temporarily until a room opened up for her in one of the newer barracks. By this time all the females had moved out of the Tin Hut, and since Becky was by herself, it didn't make much sense to tie up one whole set of bathrooms in our place just for her. Becky turned out to be a sweetheart and fit in well with all the rest of us old curmudgeons. We all pretty much took her under our wings and tried to look out for her, even though we knew she was a big girl in her own right and had military experience in Iraq.

Surfer Boy must have sniffed something in the air because he showed up around our fire pit that first evening, after Becky had joined us there. Surfer Boy, who never gave any of us the time of day and who had a reputation for being very hard to find, had never before joined our nightly ritual. He made sure that Becky knew he had an opening as a firearms instructor if she was interested, and that he could use her with his group of instructors. It was no surprise to any of us, and we were pretty certain he'd be hanging around like a tom cat from then on, but as I said, Becky was a big girl and could take care of herself.

Becky had actually been in the military police and her unit had been assigned to the Baghdad Police Academy back in 2003–04, so she was well acquainted with the place, though she had never met Surfer Boy during her previous stay. She had completed her enlistment and returned to America, and then decided to apply for an instructor job with ICITAP, this time at a much higher salary. Who could blame her? After all, for the most part that's why we were all in Iraq.

Becky was initially assigned to be teamed up with Wallie. According to him, the first day she showed up in class the reaction from the cadets was noticeable. They sat up straighter in their chairs and seemed much more attentive. During breaks they almost fell over themselves trying to be the one to hold the door open for Becky as she stepped outside of the classroom. My guess is there were a few who sucked in their guts as well. Later that day, after class, Wallie stopped me as I was walking across the compound.

"How much do we charge for our women?" he asked, with a wry smile on his face.

"What in the hell are you talking about?" I said, looking at him quizzically.

Wallie explained to me that during one of the class breaks he had been approached by two cadets who asked, through the interpreter, "How much to buy her?" Apparently, they wanted to know what the price would be to purchase Miss Becky at some point in the future. I guess once they graduated from the academy and became full-fledged

Iraqi police, flush with money, they would be looking for a wife, and Miss Becky suited them just fine. What was surprising is that only two cadets approached Wallie. My guess is that they were probably the two who drew the short straws and had to check the price for everybody else and negotiate a deal. As a courtesy to Becky, we shared the information with her and she laughed about it. Little did she know that we were all discussing among ourselves just how much we might be able to get. Just kidding!

CHAPTER 16

Promoted Right Out of a Job

Work continued to follow pretty much the same routine for all of us. Morning roll call was followed by a break, where the class would be turned over to an Iraqi Police cadre for drill and marching for an hour. Then it was back to the classroom for about another hour before breaking for lunch. Time was also factored in each week for firearms training at the range. Considering that the vetting of the cadets left something to be desired, being around them when they held loaded weapons wasn't high on my list of favorite things to do. It was only reasonable to be concerned, considering all of the 'insider shootings' that the U.S. military had experienced over the years in Iraq and Afghanistan.

While having dinner in the chow hall one day, the assistant director sat down across from me. Hitchins had been a Scottish police officer for around 20 years. We started chatting and exchanging information about our backgrounds and experiences, and about work at the academy in general. He mentioned that there were a number of management positions up for grabs, including in human resources. What they had in mind wasn't your traditional human resources position you might see back in the States. The title of 'Operations Manager/Jack of all Trades/ Chief Go-fer' would have been a more appropriate title. I mentioned that although I did not have actual HR experience, I had worked closely with the HR department in a previous life. Hitchins asked if I thought I might be interested in the academy's position. They were looking for someone who would come in and get a handle on who was assigned to the academy, and more importantly what they were actually doing. It was suspected that there were a number of 'instructors' who had never set foot in a classroom or actually taught a class, but continued to draw a huge salary for just sitting around and loafing.

Accountability was important, not just from a safety standpoint, but also to ensure that people were actually doing what they were hired and paid to do. Hitchins told me that the job was mine if I wanted it, as long as the director signed off on the deal. Malcolm had been out of town, but once back, having someone fill the responsibilities as HR manager was on the top of his priority list. As it turned out, Hitchins spoke with Malcolm that evening over the phone and mentioned our conversation. The next day, Hitchins sought me out and told me that Malcolm had given him the okay to put me in the position starting immediately. Little did I suspect that I would come to rue the day I accepted the job.

I was a little apprehensive at first, but I decided it might be just the opportunity I was looking for to hopefully make some positive changes at the academy. Plus, it would put someone from our group into a position to look out for us all. Up until that point in time, we had been pushed around by others, lied to, and deceived. Having one of us in an inside position might help us get better and more accurate information about the program, and what was going on at the Baghdad Police Academy in particular.

Once Malcolm had returned from his trip home to Scotland I got to meet him for the first time, I liked him immediately. His accent was heavy, but he seemed like a really decent guy and was genuinely interested in trying to oversee a good program. He followed up on what I had been told by Hitchins—there was some question as to who was actually still at the academy because people sometimes came and went without the administration knowing about it. Malcolm was concerned about accountability from a safety standpoint, but also out of a sense of integrity for the program. He simply did not want a bunch of 'instructors' getting paid big bucks for sitting around and doing absolutely nothing. And obviously, if an emergency evacuation was ordered we had to know who was there so that no one got left behind by accident. Worse than that, if one of us was on the receiving end of an incoming mortar round, it would be difficult to identify us from the red smudge that was left behind if we didn't know for sure who was actually there.

I should mention that once I took over my position as HR manager, it was immediately obvious that many of those who had arrived before my group took a disliking to my promotion. I suspect many were thinking, 'Who the hell does this new guy think he is?' One of the old-timers, Bryan LaFave, congratulated me right away, but his comments meant little to me. I had determined upon first meeting him that he was not someone to trust. Many of the others gave me the cold shoulder, since word quickly spread that I had been tasked by Malcolm with the 'accountability project'. Some people, like the Triple T guys, had been collecting a pay check and doing absolutely nothing for quite a while. So naturally they were a little defensive around me. I had been tasked with bringing the 'gravy train' to an end.

I also immediately started looking for ways to improve the quality of life for my colleagues. I tackled the toilet paper issue right away. If I could solve that problem, life would be more bearable for us all. I began to look for other ways to make improvements, and to establish the accountability that Malcolm and Hitchins were looking for.

I was given an office in the AA Building, and that is where I met Hidma and Achteel, the Iraqi translators who worked out of my office. Both would become good friends of mine. Hidma was an attractive young Shia Muslim girl of 24 who spoke very good English. She wore the Muslim veil covering her hair but otherwise dressed in modest Western clothes. She always brightened my day with her smile when I arrived at the office for the day. She was genuinely a very pleasant personality and would eventually become a life-long friend, almost more of a daughter.

Achteel, also a Shia, spoke good English as well and he also liked American music. When I plugged in my little stereo he and I could jam together. Hidma would just put her earphones on and listen to Arab music. Both were very pleasant to work with and extremely helpful. Hidma seemed to be really interested in American culture and we would chat often about any number of topics related to life in the United States. Even though she worked at the Iraqi police academy she had nothing good really to say about the IP. Growing up under the regime of Saddam Hussein, she told me they did not have a good reputation, especially the police commandos, basically the Iraqi version of a SWAT team. They were considered to be nothing more than criminal thugs in uniform.

Hidma and I developed something of a game, where she would approach me with some slang expression or saying such as, 'Why the long face?' or 'Going to hell in a hand-basket' and ask me what they meant. I would try to give her the meaning and the history of these colloquialisms as best I could. After a while it got to where I would bring her a new one in for the day, and we'd exchange expressions and their definitions. It became a regular routine between us and it was a lot of fun.

Achteel always tried to have the coffee pot ready for me in the morning, which was much appreciated. At lunch time each day I would leave and go to the chow hall to grab a bite to eat. I started smuggling lunch back to the HR office to share with Hidma and Atheel, staying away from pork. As previously mentioned, the food at every meal was great, especially the desserts. I was able to treat Hidma and Achteel to pastries, slices of pie or cake, and other items that they simply couldn't find in the local Iraqi economy, and they were always very appreciative. A close friendship quickly developed between us and has continued ever since. Looking back, I would have to say that the friendships I made with Hidma and Achteel, but especially Hidma, are probably the only good things to come out of our nation's long involvement in Iraq, at least as far as I'm concerned.

Achteel also volunteered to obtain items that we couldn't get because of the danger involved in leaving the protection of the academy compound. On one occasion, I had seen an Iraqi translator wearing a gold chain around her neck, with a small gold charm shaped like Iraq in the colors of the Iraqi flag. I thought it was cool and would make a good gift, so I asked Achteel if he could get me one. In just a few days he showed up for work with one, which had cost him roughly $100. It was much less than I would have paid, if I could have even gotten out and made the purchase. Achteel could do just about anything asked of him. He was handy around the office, making minor repairs or at least getting something handled fairly quickly if he couldn't fix it himself.

After taking on my new responsibilities, I contacted the Adnan Palace to see if I could get an accurate roster count of who was actually assigned to the academy, and in what capacity. I was surprised to hear that the information wasn't readily available. It seemed that no one over in the Green Zone had such a roster to hand. With people coming and going all the time, it seemed to me that this information should be right at someone's fingertips, and I couldn't believe there was no accurate, up-to-the-minute record of who was where as part of the ICITAP program. I'm sure someone somewhere must have had the information, but no one I spoke to could provide me with a roster. I viewed this as a somewhat disconcerting situation. If the compound had come under attack, we would have no way of knowing if everyone had been safely evacuated. It was critical to ensure that no one was left behind by accident.

This was a common problem with ICITAP in Baghdad—too many chiefs and not enough Indians. There were so many titled positions running around the Green Zone with ICITAP, and so much schmoozing going on with the army and the U.S. Embassy. ICITAP people were constantly currying favor with higher-ranking officials, and important work didn't seem to be a priority for them. It was more important to be hanging out at the pool behind Saddam's Green Zone palace.

I soon discovered that there were several instructors at the academy who were quite happy with the way things were. Anonymity afforded them the opportunity to do just about whatever they wanted, with little or no accountability. Some people were getting paid large sums of money to work on their suntan, play poker, sleep late, and anything else they could do to avoid actually working.

Hitchins asked me one day to visit the offices of the Triple T (Train The Trainer) guys and see if I could find out how much progress was being made in terms of training Iraqis to train themselves.

"Karl is running the Triple Ts," Hitchins said. "See if he's there and find out where they are with their program." That alone sounded a little ominous to me—the assistant director didn't know what some of his own people were actually doing.

The Triple Ts were supposed to be teaching Iraqis to be instructors for themselves, so that eventually they could take over the police academy training programs and put all of us out of a job. As I entered their office, I saw three or four Iraqis working away at desks inside. I asked one of them, "Is Karl in? Where can I find him?" All the Iraqis looked at me with blank expressions. After inquiring further, the one closest to me said, "We don't really know where Mr. Karl is. We don't often see him." It seemed that Karl only occasionally stopped by the Triple T offices to check in with his Iraqi staff.

The rest of the officers assigned to the Triple T program were pretty much unknown to the Iraqis who worked there. It seems they were never around much and no one really knew who they were, what they looked like, or even how many of them there were. I was advised that Karl might be at the Blue Lagoon barracks, so I walked over to see what I could find out. As I approached, I noticed right away that there was an instructor stretched out on a lounge chair, taking in some rays. Another instructor was sitting inside his room with the door open, reading some papers. I approached him.

"I'm looking for Karl," I asked. "Are you Karl?" The man looked up at me.

"Yeah," he replied. "Who's asking?"

At this point, the sunbathing instructor took notice and propped himself up on one elbow, watching the exchange while sipping from a bottle of water. I introduced myself to Karl.

"I'm the new HR guy," I said. "Malcolm asked me to find you and check where things are on the Triple T program. I stopped over at your office but the Iraqis there said they hadn't seen you today."

Karl became a little defensive and immediately replied, "I go to the office," as though I was questioning whether he put any time in there at all. He then added, "I'll talk to Malcolm."

"Ok, thanks," I replied, as I turned and walked away.

It was obvious to me that there was something going on, I just wasn't sure what it was. In fairness, the Triple T instructors might have been doing a bang-up job, but it wasn't apparent to the academy director or even to their own Iraqi staff. It certainly appeared that not a whole lot of effort was being made by the Triple T guys to do much of anything. For $13,075 dollars a month, they were at least getting a nice suntan.

I headed back to my office for a cup of coffee and to ponder my next steps. Oftentimes my new role felt more like a fireman than a policeman. I put out fires all day.

As mentioned, one of my first orders of business was to try to improve the living conditions at the academy. The toilet paper issue turned out to be pretty easy to fix. All I had to do was contact the Iraqi 'logistics' person. I found him near a storage building full of huge boxes of toilet paper. When I asked him what I needed to do to get more of it delivered he responded, "I need someone from academy management to sign for it." I figured that was me, so I pulled out my pen, smiled and held it up for him to see. It's amazing what a signature on a piece of paper would do for the Iraqis. After decades of living under a brutal dictatorship, no one wanted to take responsibility for anything in case they might be held accountable. Under Saddam, that could mean paying not only with your life, but your family's lives as well.

I told the guy to supply six rolls of toilet paper for each toilet, every single day. That equaled 18 rolls for the men's three toilets. At first he looked at me like I was crazy, but I explained that there were over 30 people using the toilets in the Tin Hut each day, and my signature did the trick. I probably have an outstanding bill under my name for a thousand rolls of toilet paper, in addition to the sack full of pillows. From that day forward, each toilet had six rolls of toilet paper every single day. That alone went a long way towards improving morale and making life in the Tin Hut a little more bearable. People no longer had to have family members mailing them boxes of toilet paper from home.

Next were the showers, which still leaked all over the floor whenever they were used. I looked to Tackleberry for help with this, since he was fairly handy at doing things. I asked if he could lower the curtain rods about three inches, so the curtains would fit inside the bottom of the stalls. I also told him to spread the word to everyone to make sure to keep the curtains inside the stall instead of hanging outside. This helped alleviate one of the big points of irritation—having to slosh around through inch-deep water in order to use the shower or just take a dump. I'm sure there were some health-related issues that were probably addressed as well. It was such a simple solution to the problem, I was surprised it hadn't been sorted out before. Naturally there were some people who just didn't get it, and would just let the curtain hang wherever it fell, not even trying to keep it inside the stall. When they showered you had to stand by with the squeegee, but for the most part everyone cooperated and it helped keep the shower room much drier.

I found that sometimes, actually most of the time, there were very simple solutions to our problems. Things that people bitched and moaned about often turned out to have really simple solutions, but nobody wanted to take ownership of a problem and fix it. They'd rather piss and moan about something and say 'woe is me.'

Also funny was how the complainers almost seemed to resent it when a problem was solved. It was as though one of their favorite 'bitches' had been taken away from them, so they'd need to find something else to bitch about. I think there may also have been some sheepishness involved—a simple solution had been staring them in the face all the time and they either never recognized it, or didn't take steps to fix it themselves. It's human nature that people don't like to have their faults or failings pointed out to them, even in a subtle way. I certainly don't, and I have my fair share.

In my role as a 'fireman', putting out fires around the compound, I dealt with one situation that had the potential to erupt into actual gunfire between two instructors. All of us appreciated the care packages that we received from back home—usually they were full of things we had either requested, or things our families thought we might like to have. Often they included items that we simply could not get in Iraq. Sometimes we would get home-baked cookies, and Baghdad Boob once got an inflatable sheep from his former colleagues back in the States, presumably for those lonely Baghdad nights.

One day, Mitch was away from the room he shared with Dudley when the mail was delivered, which included a package for Mitch. Dudley sat there staring at the unopened package until he simply couldn't stand the anticipation any longer. He went ahead and opened it to see what was inside. The package contained some home-baked cookies from Mitch's wife, so Dudley decided to help himself, consuming most, if not all, of the cookies.

When Mitch returned to the room, Dudley gave him his package and let him know he had opened it and helped himself to the cookies inside. Mitch went ballistic. The next thing I know, I'm getting visited in my room by several colleagues, telling me that I'd better do something quickly or Mitch was going to beat Dudley into a pulp. One might argue that Mitch would have been justified.

Afterwards, Mitch told me that a storm had been brewing from the very first day they ended up in a room together. Dudley was apparently a real pain in the ass, a little busybody, always looking over Mitch's shoulder, sticking his nose into Mitch's business, and generally being a pest. Mitch had put up with about all that he could handle, and the cookies incident was the final straw. Dudley appeared to not even realize that what he'd done was pretty un-cool. He thought Mitch and he were good buddies and opening Mitch's package from home was no big deal. In his mind, what was Mitch's was also his.

Since there was a room coming available in one of the older Blue Lagoon barracks across the compound, I pulled some strings and got it assigned to Mitch, in order to get him away from Dudley. Another fire put out.

CHAPTER 17

Morale Phone? What Morale Phone?

One day while walking across the academy compound I was approached by Ruby, who had a look of consternation on her face.

"Del, have you heard of the morale phone?" she asked me.

I stood there with a dumbfounded look on my face, not knowing what she was talking about.

"Morale phone?" I replied. "What the hell is a moral phone?"

Ruby informed me that there was apparently a cell phone floating around the academy, provided by the ICITAP program and intended to allow the instructors to get in touch with family back home. The morale phone was nothing more than a normal cell phone, which you could purchase at the PX in the Green Zone, but it was supplied with pretty much unlimited minutes to use each month. Apparently, everyone at the academy was supposed to have equal access to it. I told Ruby I would look into it. When I got back to my office in the AA Building, I stopped by to see Hitchins and asked him about this so-called morale phone.

In his Scottish accent, Hitchins replied, "Yes, there's a cell phone provided by ICITAP for you all to use. I think maybe Carly or Arnie can tell you where it is."

I thanked Hitch and went looking for either Arnie or Carly to find out just where this morale phone was. I walked over to the new barracks, which Arnie's group had inhabited after leaving the Tin Hut, and bumped into Carly coming out the door.

"Carly, what's this 'morale phone' thing I'm hearing about?" I asked.

A look of terror momentarily crossed her face as Carly stuttered and stammered for a few seconds. She finally answered, "I'm not sure, ask Arnie."

"Well, what exactly is this morale phone anyway?' I asked. "We've never heard of it."

Carly finally confirmed that it did in fact exist, and that they had been passing it back and forth amongst themselves, using it to call back home to family and friends. It was obvious to my trained investigator's eye that Carly and her little clique had been keeping this phone to themselves and not sharing it with others, 'bogarting' the phone, so to speak. The fewer people who knew about its existence, the fewer people they had to share it with. It was another example of why certain people just didn't belong. In a war zone you don't just look out for yourself, you should have the back of the person next to you. You share the burdens and share the benefits equally.

All of us had purchased cell phones at the Green Zone PX when we first arrived in Baghdad. You could load up with minutes from 'pay-as-you-go' scratch cards, purchased separately at your own expense. The cards had a serial number, which would automatically add minutes to your phone that you could then use to call home. Cellular service wasn't perfect in Baghdad, but it was reliable enough that you could fairly regularly call home and speak with family members. Having one provided by ICITAP, free of charge, would save all of us a few bucks, and being isolated from the Green Zone PX meant we weren't always able to get our hands on the scratch cards to reload our own phones when they ran out of minutes.

I guess it's the old cop blood in me, but nothing pisses me off more than people who try to 'get over' on others. And that is exactly what it looked like was going on. Carly and Arnie's little clique had gotten hold of this morale phone and decided to just keep it among themselves.

"Tell Arnie or whoever has the phone to get hold of me," I said. "We need to come up with a roster and a schedule to ensure that *everyone* has the opportunity to use it."

I detected a brief dirty look coming from Carly, but then she smiled and said, "Sure, no problem. I'll see who has it and have them give it to you."

I thought to myself, we'll see how long that takes, but it showed up later that evening (my bet was that Carly had the phone herself). I quickly drew up a schedule so that everyone would have an equal opportunity to use it. Each person would sign for it when they picked it up, so we could keep track of who had it last in order to ensure it didn't disappear again.

Another fire had been put out.

CHAPTER 18

The Seven Dead Puppies Saloon

The orders from the military were clear—mongrel dogs running loose in Baghdad were not to be taken in as pets. They were flea-infested and potentially disease-carrying menaces. Soldiers were instructed to shoot them on sight if they were discovered inside the police academy compound. Those of us who were dog lovers had some difficulty with this, but most of us understood the necessity, for health and sanitation reasons. Veterinary services were non-existent in Iraq, and no one could tell what kind of diseases these feral animals might be capable of transmitting.

One day, Stan's wife Ruby approached me, obviously upset about something.

"You won't believe what they've done now," she exclaimed as she got in front of me. Ruby didn't have to tell me who 'they' were, I knew it had to be Katherine and Carly. Ruby was not getting along with them and there was a definite personality conflict. "They've got a dog in the women's shower room. Not just a dog, but a bitch with seven puppies! There's crap and piss everywhere!"

Ruby was beside herself. Apparently, she had discovered this by accident when she walked into the shower room, noticed the horrible smell, and immediately stepped into a pile of dog shit. Needless to say, she wasn't the least bit happy about it, and understandably so. I calmed her down and told her I'd look into it.

After she left, I walked over to the barracks to check it out for myself. When I walked inside I could immediately detect a foul smell coming from the women's bathroom. Just to be on the safe side and not walk in on any female who had just stepped out of the shower, I announced myself loudly before walking all the way inside the shower area. I was answered by the yipping of puppies but nothing else. Once I walked in, I could see the mother laying on the floor while seven puppies crawled around the shower room. The floor was covered with dog shit and urine. It looked and smelled disgusting. No wonder Ruby was pissed off—it was a situation that had to be dealt with.

Apparently, Katherine and Carly had discovered the mother and her puppies wandering the compound and decided to protect them. So they'd scooped the dogs up and taken them to their barracks, stashing them inside the women's bathroom. Since neither Katherine nor Carly were around, I walked over to the AA Building and into Malcolm's office. When I explained the situation he got visibly angry.

"Get those beasts out of that barracks now!" he shouted, but then added, "Wait, I'll take care of it."

I left his office convinced that Katherine and Carly's 'kennel' would soon be dealt with, and when I saw Ruby shortly thereafter she informed me that the problem had indeed been solved. Katherine and Carly gave me the stink-eye every time I crossed paths with them after this. They held me responsible for what happened, I guess, and I'm sure they were thinking I was a dog killer!

In a somewhat related matter, there was a female company commander in the military police unit assigned to the academy who was also a dog lover. The story goes that while she was on leave back in America she did a kind of a 'local girl does good' type of interview for the local media. During this interview, she mentioned feeling bad for the poor dogs running free all over Baghdad, and in the Baghdad Police Academy in particular, and the way they had to scrounge for whatever food scraps they could find.

At some point after she returned to Camp Shield, she was called into the 1st Cav battalion commander's office and told that dozens of 50-pound bags of dog food had been delivered to her unit, apparently sent by sympathetic dog lovers back in the U.S. who had read her interview. Obviously, the battalion commander wasn't happy with having all these bags of dog food taking up space, as well as the fact that having it around would encourage soldiers to feed the mongrel dogs and contribute to the potential health problems associated with them. She was told to get rid of it immediately. I'm not sure how she accomplished that task, but when you're in the army and your colonel tells you to do something, you get it done quickly. I happened to be walking across the 1st Cav part of the compound around this time and saw this woman as she was leaving the commander's office. She appeared to be visibly shaken and upset, which lends credence to the story.

Another issue of concern involved our mail deliveries. Originally we received our mail via the 1st Cav—there was an APO (American Post Office) assigned to the unit at Camp Shield. When they moved out, however, they not only took their chow hall, they also took the APO, so other arrangements had to be made for everyone left at the academy.

After some discussion, it was decided that our incoming mail could be picked up at the Rusafa Prison, which was located adjacent to the academy. There were American corrections instructors working there, who received regular mail deliveries, brought from the Green Zone. Our incoming mail could be delivered to them and we could pick it up from there, since there was only a street separating the prison from the academy and it was fairly safe to drive there, although you still had to gear up in body armor and Kevlar helmet just to go this short distance.

At Rusafa, though, they did not have any outgoing mail service, since they made regular trips to the Green Zone for other business and could send outgoing mail on those occasions. Our movements were much more restricted than theirs, so instead our outgoing mail was couriered over to the military's FOB at Camp Cuervo in Rustimya, several miles away. Camp Cuervo had a full-service APO facility that we could use to send mail. Malcolm decided that I should be the one to do the outgoing mail runs once a week, and this turned into a huge nightmare for me.

Each week I would let people know what day I would be making the mail run. I would then collect all the outgoing mail from everyone at the academy, which always included many packages with gifts and souvenir items. Carly and Katherine in particular were always sending gifts and other things they had picked up back to America. It was up to me to transport these packages via a PSD trip over to the APO on Camp Cuervo. I had to carry the packages along with the necessary money for postage and insurance. After mailing all the packages, I would then have to bring receipts and change back to the academy, and trying to keep it all straight was a challenge in and of itself. No one ever had exact money, because they never knew exactly how much the postage for their package was going to be. On top of it all, I was the one who was risking getting blown up by an IED or shot up in an ambush, just so someone could mail a stuffed animal to a friend back home.

Until the army finally stopped it, people were always mailing back bayonets for the AK-47. It seems there was a whole garage full of them at the academy, purchased from the Soviet Union by the Saddam Hussein regime years earlier. The U.S. Army did not allow the sending back of 'war trophies' or things like that, but for some reason they viewed these bayonets differently, since they weren't actually considered 'war trophies'. They were given away free to anyone who wanted one, so all the instructors were sending them back for themselves, or to friends and family, as souvenirs. Most people just wrapped some paper around a bayonet, put an address on it and then sent it on its way, with me serving as the mail man.

My first mail run to Camp Cuervo was actually pretty uneventful, though as usual we careened around the streets of Baghdad, shoving cars out of the way, driving up onto curbs and sidewalks, doing anything to keep from having to stop our convoy. When you came to a stop you became a much easier target for any bad guys who might be hanging around the roundabouts and other natural choke points, waiting for an opportunity.

Sometimes during these mail runs, I had 15 or 20 packages. Some of them were simply outlandish, like large rolled-up Persian carpets. There was also the problem of the APO personnel inspecting the packages to make sure that no contraband or other prohibited items were being sent home—like weapons or hand grenades. So after loading up and hauling all the outgoing packages to Camp Cuervo, they had to be inspected before I could seal them up and have them weighed to find out the postage costs. Of course, everybody wanted insurance on their packages, so I had to fill out the insurance paperwork as well. Then I had to keep all the paperwork and change for each package separate and correct.

As I said, it was a royal pain in the ass, and not just for me. The poor soldiers at Camp Cuervo hated to see me show up on the mail run. They might have a single item to mail home but would have to stand in line forever waiting for me to finish up. It could take a very long time if only one mail clerk was working because someone was on lunch break, which was often the case. It seemed that our convoy always arrived at Camp Cuervo around lunch time.

I tried to be courteous to the soldiers, since I knew they often they had a limited amount of time to take care of personal business. I would work diligently on trying to mail my packages, but I would stop occasionally and allow a soldier to step up to the counter and mail his item before I resumed. Obviously, this added to the amount of time it took for me to complete the outgoing mail run.

On one run I was treated to the 'great mud puddle diving competition'. We parked our vehicles at Camp Cuervo, not far from the APO mail room, next to a huge mud puddle about 15 feet long by 10 feet wide. Its depth was unknown, but was probably no more than six or eight inches. One of the soldiers from our convoy, a young sergeant, bet everyone that he would belly flop into the puddle if we got the price up to a hundred dollars or more. The money was raised in a matter of minutes, as no one really believed the soldier would carry through. But suddenly he stripped off his outer shirt in preparation. We all stood there watching as he took a few steps backwards and then charged towards the puddle and leapt into it, doing a perfect belly flop into the soupy mix.

Fortunately there were no chunks of metal with jagged edges or hidden rocks concealed under the muddy water. The soldier made a big splash as he hit, and then he very quickly jumped up again, completely covered in mud. He was shivering as well, since the muddy water was icy cold. He then ran over to a nearby barracks and walked, fully clothed, into one of the showers to clean the mud off himself and his uniform. When he returned he was soaking wet, but at least his uniform wasn't covered in mud anymore. And he was $100 richer.

One benefit of going on the mail run was that there was a small PX on Camp Cuervo, so naturally I would also volunteer to pick up some items. This started to become something of a pain in the ass too, since once again I had to keep people's orders straight and their money and change correct—everybody gave me $20 bills. It became a freaking nightmare trying to keep it all straight!

People asked for a lot of creature comforts, but in some cases they wanted absolute necessities that they couldn't get at the academy. Orders for bags of potato chips, Doritos and candy bars topped my shopping list, as well as microwave popcorn! I'd leave the academy on a mail run with a shopping list from a dozen or more people, in addition to all the mail, and they were always concerned about getting the correct change back from their purchases.

I would put an instructors' money in an envelope with their name on it so I could keep things straight, but it was a very labor intensive process and sometimes mistakes were made. Sometimes a package didn't get mailed, left by accident in the back of the Humvee, or some items ordered from the PX would be forgotten. Naturally I took the heat for any mistakes, but the other instructors had no clue what a process it all was. They'd get pissed off if they didn't get exactly what they wanted or if I lost or forgot to bring them a receipt back.

On one particular day, Malcolm asked me to do the mail run as there was a meeting at the academy that he wanted me to attend for him. Jimmy 'Two Dogs' had no classes that day, so he volunteered to make the run in my stead. I sat down with him before the trip to go over what needed to be done and how to keep track of everything, and he assured me that he was on top of things.

Jimmy made the run without incident and returned after a few hours, but prior to leaving he informed me that his good friend Jerry was arriving at the academy sometime that day. Jimmy had enticed his friend out of retirement to come over to Iraq. They had served together as U.S. customs investigators for quite a few years and were close friends. Jerry hadn't been keen on coming over to Iraq, but Jimmy had told him about the money and that it was a good gig to work on, so Jerry had relented. I told Jimmy I'd take care of Jerry when he arrived and make sure he got settled in.

When Jerry's PSD arrived, I walked over to find him. On the spur of the moment, I decided it would be a good idea to screw with Jerry, even though I didn't know him at all. I figured any friend of Jimmy's was fair game, plus it was sort of a tradition at the academy to mess with the new guys. I walked up and introduced myself and asked if he was Jimmy's friend. Jerry was looking around trying to locate Jimmy when he answered me.

"Yes, I'm Jerry," he said. "Where's Jimmy?"

Completely unrehearsed and off the top of my head, I made up a story.

"I'm not sure what's going on," I said. "Jimmy was picked up earlier this morning by the MPs and I guess he's probably over in the Green Zone. I think he's being detained in their custody for some reason. I'm not really sure, but it might have something to do with him stealing gas from military vehicles to start our nightly camp fires. Jimmy's been crawling underneath parked Humvees each night and stealing a little fuel from them. One of the soldiers might have seen him and reported him."

Jerry appeared deflated. He had traveled to Iraq just to work with his buddy, only to find that he'd been arrested and would likely be sent home, maybe in handcuffs, leaving poor Jerry behind. As we walked towards the Tin Hut, where Jerry would be billeted, we passed a few other people and I would say, "It's a shame about Jimmy isn't it?", to which each of them would reply, "Yeah, what a shame." They didn't have a clue what I was talking about, but they fell in line since they knew some kind of scam was being played on the new guy. Once they got past us I'm sure they started chuckling to themselves.

I got Jerry fixed up with a room and had him drop his gear and luggage off. By this time it was later in the day, so we just went outside and sat down around the fire pit waiting for the chow hall to open up. Jerry sat there with this forlorn look on his face, silently considering his dilemma and trying to decide what to do. I'm sure he was also wondering and worrying about his friend Jimmy.

A short while later, Jimmy returned from the mail run and saw his friend standing around outside, still looking down in the dumps. My little scam had lasted the whole day. No one had given the game away and Jerry had never caught on. He still thought his buddy was in serious trouble.

As he was casually walking up to the Tin Hut, Jimmy called out, "Hey Jerry, what's up? Get settled in?" as if nothing had happened, which of course it hadn't. Jerry was flummoxed, not expecting to see his buddy Jimmy and certainly not expecting him to be so casual after having been carted off by the MPs earlier in the day. They stared at each other for a few seconds and then those of us sitting there who were in on the scam started laughing.

The story finally came out about what we had done to Jerry. I have to admit that he was pretty good about it all. He learned a very valuable lesson on his first day at the academy—that we were all full of shit most of the time. Jimmy loved it too. Welcome to the Baghdad Police Academy, Jerry.

There was a secondary issue that came out of Jimmy's mail run, which caused a bit of consternation for a few days. Katherine and Carly had sent a couple of packages, but by accident they didn't get mailed, remaining inside their mail sack in the back of the vehicle. When Jimmy returned, the women approached him for their change and receipts. When Jimmy acted confused, they began demanding the receipts for postage and the insurance, but Jimmy couldn't produce them. He gave them money back but had no receipts for the postage or insurance costs. Both girls went whining to Malcolm, wanting to file federal criminal charges against Jimmy for 'theft of mail' and 'mail fraud'.

It was a completely ridiculous and childish reaction, exactly what I had come to expect from these two. They flew off the handle without taking the time to find out what had happened and immediately thought a major crime had been committed, which speaks to the fact that neither of them had any police experience or knowledge of the law. Rule number one is to know what laws are supposed to have been broken, and rule number two is to conduct an investigation to look for any evidence that a crime has actually been committed. Preferably before you start accusing someone.

I spoke with Malcolm and told him I'd try to sort it all out, but there were no criminal violations anywhere. I told him Katherine and Carly were overreacting to something that likely had a very simple explanation. I got back with Jimmy and asked him what had happened to Katherine and Carly's packages. He had no clue, insisting he had mailed all the packages that he'd taken with him.

The animosity that had developed between the different groups had started to spill over. Carly and Katherine decided to pursue it up the line to the senior leadership in the Green Zone, complaining that Jimmy had stolen their mail. They actually wanted criminal charges to be filed, though I'm sure they had no clue what particular crime had been committed, other than the generic 'mail theft'.

After a few days, the head of the PSD unit came to my office with a couple of items they had found in the back of their vehicle. Katherine and Carly's packages had somehow gotten separated from the rest of the mail the day Jimmy made the mail run. I decided then and there that I was fed up with Katherine and Carly's whining and game-playing, so I hung onto the packages in my office and sent them when I made the next mail run. After I returned, I gave them receipts for the postage and insurance, making sure I smeared the dates on both so that they were unreadable. I told them Jimmy had found the receipts tucked inside a pocket in his body armor where he had stashed them. He had just discovered them and given them to me. Naturally, I filled in Jimmy so that our stories would match. They still didn't want to believe me, so I told them to let me know if the packages they mailed didn't show up and they wanted to collect insurance on them. I made sure that they understood that trying to collect insurance money on packages that had been received was also a very serious crime. They were still convinced that Jimmy and I had conspired together to screw with them, but I'm guessing their packages finally showed up, since I never heard another word from them. And as far as I know they never tried to collect any insurance.

Following the conclusion of the 'Great Mail Caper', I was walking across the grounds towards the Blue Lagoon barracks one day when I heard and actually felt a huge explosion off in the distance. It was a massive blast, and pieces of debris started falling into the academy compound. Maybe a mile away, a large plume of black smoke could be seen reaching up into the sky. Obviously, it got everyone's attention. I overheard one of the other instructors yell out "Get some!" in response to the blast, and while most cops aren't a stranger to gallows humor I couldn't help but think that very likely someone, or perhaps many people, had just gotten blown to bits—I just hoped no Americans had been involved. It didn't seem funny or something to cheer about to me, but I guess we all deal with tragic situations differently. It was later on that we found out it had been a massive VBIED (Vehicle-Borne IED), which had tried to hit the Al Sadeer Hotel, where some of the ICITAP employees were being billeted.

We learned that a large garbage truck, laden with explosives, had entered the compound. The Iraqi guard, apparently recognizing it for what it was, had opened fire on the truck driver. The driver was holding a 'dead man's switch', which allowed the vehicle to explode even if he was killed. The truck had come to a stop just short of the building when the device activated.

All the windows on one side of the hotel were blown out. Many of the vehicles parked alongside the hotel were also destroyed and set ablaze, and a number of people were hurt inside the hotel, especially in the rooms that were facing the explosion. When the shooting started, they had looked out of their windows to see what was going on, and many of them received injuries when their windows were shattered by the explosion.

The Iraqi guard who opened fire on the truck was killed by the blast, but he saved many American lives by his actions. Had the truck gotten right up next to the building, it very likely would have collapsed the entire hotel, causing massive loss of life, much like what happened at the federal building in Oklahoma City years earlier.

Along with the regular mortar attacks, the ambushes of PSDs, incoming rocket fire striking the Blue Lagoon barracks, and the spent AK-47 rounds piercing the roof of the Tin Hut, this massive explosion was just another reminder of how tenuous our lives were at that time. We were in a war zone, and Baghdad was 'Jihadi Central' in 2004–5.

Needless to say, the instructors who were living at the Al Sadeer Hotel had to find new lodgings.

CHAPTER 19

Carrying a Gun to Go Banking

I had to schedule another trip to the Green Zone for a doctor's appointment (a minor health issue had developed, just one of those nagging things that couldn't be addressed by the medic at the academy). Arrangements for a PSD were made for a visit to the CSH, the Coalition Surgical Hospital, located near Saddam's Palace. As it would necessitate an overnight stay, I packed a small bag with just a change of underwear and toiletries. If for some reason my stay was extended, I'd just pick up a new set of duds at the PX.

There were no problems during the PSD ride to the Green Zone, and after I was dropped off at the Adnan Palace I grabbed a vehicle and headed to the CSH for my appointment. It was something of a surreal experience. The CSH was surrounded by high concrete blast walls, sandbags, and HESCOs, and there were dozens of armed people wandering around inside—not something you would see at a hospital in America. Painted arrows on the floor directed you to the particular medical section you were visiting. I followed the yellow arrows and checked in with the nurse. After sitting around in the waiting area for a while I was met by a medical person who discussed my ailment, gave me an examination, and released me with a clean bill of health. The problem wasn't anything to be concerned about and could be taken care of once I returned home. I would just have to put up with the nagging until then.

Since I was in the Green Zone, and the military finance office was also located near the hospital, I decided to walk over and cash a personal check. If I'd thought it was surreal walking through a hospital with so many armed people, imagine standing in line at the teller's window in the finance office carrying a 9mm pistol on your hip and a fully automatic M-4 carbine slung across your shoulder, while surrounded by others standing in line who were also armed to the teeth. This was certainly not something you would see at a bank in America, unless the person carrying those weapons was also wearing a mask.

When I got to the teller, I slid my check and CAC card through the slot in the window and a minute later I was walking out of the finance office with a wad of cash in my hand, enough to last a few hands in one of the high-stakes poker games at the academy.

After leaving the finance office I headed back to my vehicle. It was a common sight on the street where I was parked to see Iraqis selling DVDs and other trinkets. On this occasion, as I walked towards my vehicle I was approached by a small Iraqi boy of maybe 10 or 11 years of age, yelling out "Porno! Porno!" I chased him away, only to have him return a few seconds later offering me first-run Hollywood movies that weren't even out on DVD back in the States. The quality of the DVDs was never very good, hence the cheap price—three or four DVDs for only five bucks. Sometimes the pirate copies had been made by setting up a video camera in the back of a theater and videotaping while the movie was playing.

If you bought one, the quality was likely to be really bad, and it might just stop half way through the movie—oftentimes only half the movie had been recorded. Needless to say, there was no way to get a refund, you were very unlikely to ever find the same Iraqi kid again, particularly since our trips to the Green Zone were few and far between. He may also have moved onto other areas, and even if you did find him, it's doubtful he'd give you your money back anyway. The good English he spoke when you bought the DVDs would have disappeared and he would suddenly only speak Arabic, and even if he did give you your money back, he would simply put the returned DVD back into his inventory and sell it to some other poor soldier.

There were businesses and restaurants operating inside the Green Zone as well, including the Chinese restaurant that I had been told to try. After all, Baghdad was still a functioning city and businesses had been allowed to reopen once the Green Zone had been cordoned off and fortified. There were Iraqi homes and apartment buildings as well. After walking down some narrow alleyways and making a few turns I finally found the restaurant. I had been told the food was good, but the absence of dogs and cats, normally very common in Baghdad, convinced me to skip dinner.

I returned to the Adnan Palace to stay in the tent once more. I hooked up with my PSD escort the next morning to return to the academy, and the trip back was as uneventful as the trip out, which was always good news—there were no explosions and I didn't get shot at.

I returned to work, only to be confronted with a problem that none of us had dealt with before. If we had learned anything in our careers as police officers, it was to expect the unexpected and always be prepared to respond to and resolve a problem, but Baghdad pushed our abilities in this area to the limit at times.

I was chatting with Ronnie (who oversaw security at the academy) outside the AA building one afternoon, following the lunch break. All of a sudden his walkie-talkie started crackling—one of the entrance guards needed help.

"Ronnie, I need you down here right away," the soldier said. "I have a group of clerics with a sheep. They want to ritually sacrifice it on the academy grounds to bless the new class of cadets."

Ronnie looked at me and just kind of shook his head and said, "Only in Baghdad." He headed towards his vehicle to drive down to the gate by Palestine Street. I'm not sure how Ronnie resolved the issue, because I got distracted by another 'fire' that had to be dealt with. As I said before, those of us charged with trying to run the academy always felt much more like firemen than police officers. Our days were filled with solving one problem after another. Keeping everyone happy was not likely, but that was the goal, and ideally problems should be resolved without killing anyone, which at times was also a real challenge.

CHAPTER 20

Wiffle Ball and Mortar Rounds

Entertaining oneself on an isolated compound in the middle of a war zone isn't the easiest thing to do. Yes, we sat around the fire pit every evening and had a few drinks and told jokes and lies to each other, but even that got old at times. The monotony sometimes got to the point where we would welcome hearing an explosion, or the sounds of a nearby ambush, as it provided a diversion and gave us something to talk about.

While surfing the internet in my room one day, I happened upon an advertisement for 'wiffle ball' sets. After the smoke from the imaginary 'lightning bolt' over my head had cleared, I fired off an order for several sets, including extra balls to replace any that might get hit over the compound wall into 'Injun territory'. They could only be retrieved if an armed combat patrol braved sniper fire, so it was better to make sure we had an extra supply in case someone at the academy challenged Babe Ruth's home run record. I was surprised to find that the business offered free delivery once they realized the order came from U.S. personnel serving in Iraq. I wasn't concerned about the price, we were making enough money to afford a few sets of wiffle balls and bats, but it was an awfully nice gesture on the part of the business.

Once I received the sets, I decided to instill a little competitive spirit between us civilians and the small MP unit still at the academy—we needed to have a challenge match. Civilian cops against the MPs. Old guys against youngsters. So I went to my office and wrote up a good-natured, yet very 'insulting' letter to the army unit, questioning their 'maleness', and basically calling them a bunch of whoopsies. I dropped it off with their first sergeant and left. It was received as intended, us old geezers challenging them to a grudge match, and the army took my letter the right way, knowing full well I was being funny and not really insulting at all. They accepted our challenge and arrangements were made for the first of several games.

Following some initial 'trash talk', revolving around us being a bunch of out-of-shape old farts—which was basically a very true statement—gameday arrived. Since we were the challengers, we took the field first and let the MPs come up to bat. I took the mound and was pitching a shutout. I gave up a couple of hits, but they were scoreless after five innings. My curveball was working well and I was getting great movement on my fastball. The young soldiers on the army team were getting pissed off at their inability to score and naturally, after all their trash talk, we were rubbing it in at every opportunity. By this point we had scored seven runs and were leading by a very comfortable margin.

Suddenly, the sound of incoming mortar rounds got our attention and everyone hit the deck. I'm not sure how much protection some small clumps of dirt and a few blades of grass afforded me, but I can guarantee you I got real small, real quick, laying down out there in that open field. You could hear the mortar rounds flying overhead and impacting several hundred meters away, off towards the Ministry of the Interior building. The MOI, along with the academy itself, were always favorite targets for the bad guys. The insurgents fired off five or six rounds and then the attack ended as suddenly as it had started, which was their usual tactic. Hit and run.

I'm not sure if they'd heard about our game, or if it was simply a coincidence, but unfortunately for me they screwed up my delivery and once the game resumed I immediately gave up five runs. We still won the game, but I had lost my shut-out. I still hold the Iraqi insurgency responsible for screwing up my ERA and costing me my shut-out game. I might have been in line for our version of a Cy Young had it not been for them. As it was, we civilians ended up back at the fire pit with an adult beverage to help celebrate our victory over the army, and the next morning I woke up with a very sore right shoulder—unfortunately there was no big-league trainer around to help me work out the soreness, which persisted for several days.

We had several more games between different teams and it served as a nice diversion from the normal routine. I don't recall what our final record was, but I think we won more than we lost. We all had a lot of fun playing and it turned out to be a great distraction, and not just for us. A young Iraqi boy who worked on the compound, probably 12 or 13 years old, would sit and watch us each day as we played. He was obviously interested in this strange game. Who knows if he had ever even seen a baseball game in his short, and likely very hard, life. I suspect there wasn't much time for recreational sports for him, in contrast to the experiences of most American kids. If anything, he might have played some pick-up soccer games in the evening after a hard day of work, but probably nothing more than that.

Finally, after seeing him sitting off to the side watching us during several games, we invited him over to come up and take a few swings at bat, which he promptly did. In fact, he leapt up as if sitting on a spring and ran over to home plate. His grin went from ear to ear and it brought matching smiles to all our faces. I'm guessing some of us thought about a young boy we had back home right about then—we had made this little Iraqi boy's day, that was for sure. I doubt if he had ever had picked up a bat before, but he tried really hard and actually hit a few of the balls thrown his way. We had scored a few points with one young Iraqi boy at least. He continued to watch most days we played and from then on we always invited him to take a few swings.

Having a few beverages was one of our regular diversions in the evening after a 'hard' day at work, but we decided we needed a bar to hang out in instead of just sitting around the fire pit. It was just another attempt to bring a little slice of home over to Iraq. There were some unoccupied buildings around the compound and we began looking for one that might be suitable. If we could find one, we could decorate it to make it seem like a real bar.

I had a friend back in the U.S. who was close friends with someone who owned an Anheuser-Busch distributorship. This guy had a warehouse full of promotional items, which he often gave away. I sent an email, asking if his friend had any stuff lying around that he might want to get rid of. If he did, we'd take whatever he could send our way. Shortly thereafter, I received a couple of large packages, full of plastic mugs, bar signs and paper banners, the kind of things we could use to make our little bar feel like home.

This eventually became the foundation for the 'Del Wilber Memorial Bar' at the Baghdad Police Academy. After I left Iraq, my friends Jimmy Two Dogs and Baghdad Boob, along with some of the others, sent me a photograph they had taken outside our little bar. That was when I found out they had named it after me. They actually made a large sign, which they hung over the entrance door. It was their way of saying 'thank you' to me, I guess, for my efforts to make their lives a little more bearable. As far as I know, I am the only American to have a bar named after him in Baghdad during the Iraq War. It is an honor I am very proud of.

CHAPTER 21

Graduation

Graduation day arrived, but unfortunately the weather was bad. It was rainy and cold, so instead of conducting the ceremony out on the parade ground, it had to be held in what was basically a large basement area of the AA Building. None of us had been through a Baghdad Police Academy graduation before, so we didn't know what to expect. I went to the classrooms to pay a visit to my old class, still being taught by my former co-instructor, Kenny. The cadets all seemed genuinely happy to see me—they still remembered me having lunch with them that day so many weeks earlier. They all wanted their photo taken with me. They weren't allowed to have their own cameras, or even a cell phone, on the academy grounds for obvious security reasons, but I guess they just wanted me to remember them. I dutifully posed for photographs with the group and with individual cadets until everyone was satisfied.

It actually gave me a nice feeling, knowing that they thought so much of me, even though I had left the class early on to take the HR position. My simple act of kindness by having lunch with them that first day had gone a long way. Despite all the billions spent over the years trying to win the 'hearts and minds' of the Iraqi people, my simple gesture went further than all the programs the government wasted tons and tons of money on. Regardless of one's heritage, ethnicity, race or creed, simple decency goes a long way. If you take the time to show respect towards people, and treat them as you would want to be treated, then you can accomplish some great things.

After excusing myself from the class, I returned to the AA building, where the ceremony would take place, and I found a group of visiting dignitaries and VIPs just milling around. There was a two-star U.S. Army general, accompanied by an entourage of other military officers, as well as some senior ICITAP people (who I avoided like the plague), and a bunch of high-ranking Iraqi Police officials. Many lower-ranking police officers were running around like the proverbial chickens with their heads cut off. Having to move the ceremony indoors because of weather had screwed everything up royally. It was obviously a lot more crowded down in the basement of the AA building than out on the large parade grounds.

Once all the people were called to their seats, the ceremony began. After some introductory comments by both the American general and an Iraqi Police general, the students were called one by one to receive their certificates of graduation. They crisply marched up to the generals, saluted, received their certificates, and then turned around and marched away. The whole ceremony lasted about an hour. Once the VIPs finished shaking hands with each other, the basement began to empty out and I left and returned to my office upstairs. It was an interesting event, not too different from my own graduation from the St. Louis Police Academy many years before. It was pretty obvious that the Iraqi cadets were happy to be finished, and they all looked proud of themselves as they marched up to get their certificates and handshakes. As I watched, I felt a little melancholy knowing that a large percentage of those graduating would probably be dead within months.

CHAPTER 22

Going Home

Dan Borotsky, the head of ICITAP over in the Green Zone, arrived at the academy for meetings with the entire instructor staff. The rumor mill had been running rampant—Borotsky was there to make changes and 'clean house'. He had a reputation as a teetotaler and didn't like the supposed free-wheeling goings-on at the academy. The fact that he had 'retired' from his job as police chief under something of a cloud was an example of the hypocrisy often encountered with ICITAP. Word was that Borotsky was going to straighten things out at the Baghdad Police Academy.

It's true that many of us did have a drink or two in the evening after work, but no one that I was aware of had ever brought discredit to the program, with the exception of two instructors who should never have been hired in the first place (and who never would have been hired had the ICITAP recruiters had done a decent job of vetting applicants. They had previously been to Baghdad as corrections instructors and had been sent home for serious misconduct. They were apparently hired right back without any questions or any background investigation. It was typical of ICITAP, the left hand not knowing what the right hand was doing.)

The misconduct of these two was actually kind of classic. They were billeted with other contractors at the Al Sadeer Hotel, about a mile or so from the academy as the crow flies. They got drunk one night and, having somehow gotten their hands on a BB gun, they climbed up onto the roof of the hotel to shoot at pigeons—a little off-duty bird hunting.

As it was nighttime, and they were running around like idiots on the roof of a building while carrying a visible weapon, one of the perimeter guards opened fire on them, mistaking them for possible insurgents. Fortunately they were unhurt, but needless to say the army and ICITAP took a dim view of their activities. Baghdad apparently was a 'no hunting zone', even for pigeons. Apart from these two, who arrived sometime after our group, there were no other disciplinary problems that I was aware of, and certainly not with the instructors from my group.

In the meeting with Borotsky, we were informed that a new contracting company would be taking over the running of the ICITAP program. He added that there would be changes made, and that each one of us would have to interview if we wanted to remain as instructors with the program. He made it quite obvious that what he viewed as unprofessional conduct was going to come to an end, and some people were going to be sent home.

Following the meeting, it was obvious to me that the writing was on the wall. Anyone who wasn't willing to plead for their job wasn't going to be allowed to stay. We'd been told that we had to request an audience with Borotsky, who would decide whether or not he wanted to interview us. After the interview, if one even took place, he would decide if he would retain us or not.

A day was set for these private meetings, and everyone interested in remaining at the academy was expected to request one. I never did. I had no intention of stroking his ego just to stay in a place that I was tired of anyway. I was ready to go home, so Borotsky wasn't going to get any satisfaction from me begging to keep my job. He was an ass and I simply wasn't going to kiss his ring and beg to stay.

I figured it was time to start packing. I spoke with one of my colleagues after he had a meeting with Borotsky and he confirmed my suspicions. Borotsky wanted you to come in with your hat in your hand and beg for your job, promise to be a good boy and never again transgress. That just wasn't my style. I had done a good job and had busted my ass to make living conditions better for my colleagues. I was basically worn out from the long days I was putting in, along with the stress of trying to deal with a couple of hundred Type A personalities. The bottom line was that I just wasn't going to go kiss Borotsky's ass to keep my job, so I refused to even ask for a meeting. I would leave on my own terms. I would work right up until the day I departed and then say goodbye to the academy, to my colleagues, and to Iraq—and if I could lob a few well-placed grenades under a few people's bunks on the way out, so much the better. Just kidding.

Since I didn't ask for a meeting, I was placed on the 'uninterested/do not offer a contract' list. I was told that arrangements would be made to transport all those who were leaving and we would hear more once those arrangements had been made. As my departure date neared, I kept busy, continuing to improve the living conditions of my colleagues, doing exactly what I had been doing from the very start. Finally, one evening, I got the word that I'd be departing the next morning on a PSD back to the Green Zone. Back in my room I packed my gear and then stepped outside to sit around the fire pit for one last night.

A number of my colleagues stopped by to offer their support and say goodbye. They seemed genuinely saddened by my departure—they recognized and appreciated my efforts on their behalf. My feelings were somewhat mixed. I was looking forward to returning home to my loved ones and to the 'normalcy' of living back in the States, but I knew I'd miss my friends and worry about their safety after I left. It's common for people who have been in a war zone to fret about the friends they leave behind, and it's not unusual for them to want to get back over to the war to be with them again. I'm sure there's a name for it but suffice to say that one develops close relationships when placed in a highly stressful, dangerous environment. Whatever it's called, it's something that stays with you for the rest of your life.

As a parting gift to the Green Zone ICITAP crowd, after sitting around the fire pit that night I grabbed a piece of burnt wood and walked over to one of the blast walls. Using the charcoal end of the stick I wrote in big letters, 'Hey Borotsky, Blow Me'. It was unprofessional, I know, but I didn't give a shit. It stayed there for quite a while after I left I was told, for everyone to see.

The next morning, as I was getting ready to load up into the PSD convoy several colleagues stopped by to give me a goodbye hug and wish me well. I'll admit to having to fight back my emotions a little, not knowing if I'd ever see any of them again. I was really touched by the thoughtfulness. Plus, it made me feel pretty good about the job I had done while I'd been there. At least the rank and file I worked with appreciated my efforts. To hell with the clique over in the Green Zone.

Fortunately, I would have a familiar face with me back at the Adnan Palace. Roy had also decided to hang it up and return home. He was really missing his two young sons, and I couldn't blame him one bit. He needed to get back to his boys. We loaded up into the SUV and headed out onto the streets of Baghdad for one last trip to the Green Zone. It was hard not to do but I refused to look back. I had convinced myself that it was time to look forward. Little did I know that I'd end up returning to Baghdad three more times over the next two years.

CHAPTER 23

Home Again, With All My Pieces

As the aircraft touched down at St. Louis's Lambert International Airport, I looked out of the window and let loose a quiet sigh of relief—back home once again, safe and sound. Soon I would be settling back into a somewhat normal life. By this time my marriage was over. It was mostly my fault (being a cop's wife isn't easy and I certainly made my share of mistakes over the years), so I wasn't sure what I was going to do, or even where I was going to live for that matter. But I knew I'd figure it all out. Overcoming the challenges I had in Iraq certainly proved that anything was possible. I had enough family and friends in the area to give me a room to stay in until I could sort out my own place.

As I entered the terminal, I briefly thought of kneeling down and kissing the floor but I thought that would look contrived and phony, so I fought off the urge. I had seen others do something similar, and though they may have been genuinely moved to do it, I thought it looked stupid, so I wasn't going to join the crowd. Suffice to say that I was happy to be back in the good ol' U.S.A.

I walked towards the nearest bank of pay phones to call for a ride. I had no cell phone, since I had left it behind when I went overseas. It's amazing how dependent we've become on them. I almost felt naked without one. No one was waiting for me at the airport and I watched with some envy as other passengers were met by loved ones, being hugged and kissed and greeted warmly by family and friends. I felt a bit melancholy and a little lonely. I was thinking about my friends and what I had left behind in Iraq, and of my uncertain future. I was divorced and my kids were grown. I guess I'd kind of hoped there would be somebody waiting for me, but I picked up the pay phone and called for a ride, and then settled down on a bench outside the front of the terminal to wait.

Almost immediately I began to experience the same feelings most combat veterans do once they leave a war—a sense of 'survivor's guilt' and of missing my colleagues. Many start making mental plans to return if at all possible, just to get back to the people they care about. Yes, you care about family and loved ones back home, but there's something special that develops between people who are placed into highly stressful situations. I was home and safe, but I had left my friends and colleagues behind in danger. It's a powerful emotion and drives many who have experienced combat and similar stressful situations to want to return. The personal relationships, both good and bad, that you develop during wartime seem somehow to be enhanced and stronger than those back home. And the memories are more vivid. We each have our 'war stories' to tell, most real, some embellished, and some that bring out emotions we usually hide deep inside ourselves.

The experiences of the past several months would soon be nothing more than vivid memories of hardships and intense moments endured, both alone and together with colleagues who became friends, and, ultimately my brothers- and sisters-in-arms. There were many, many, fond memories of laughter shared and a brotherhood borne amid hardship in the middle of a war. A thin smile creased my face as I laughed quietly to myself, thinking about some of the things that I still couldn't believe had happened. Nor would anyone else, I was sure, unless they too had lived it.

The gallows humor that cops and members of the armed forces develop as a sort of safety valve to help them deal with the tragedies they see, is very real, and it helps us keep our sanity in some very crazy times. While you may not laugh at the time something is happening, looking back on it afterwards we often find ourselves shaking our heads in wonder and laughing quietly to ourselves—or laughing heartily after a couple of beers with colleagues who lived through it too.

I had survived my courtship with danger in the Iraq War. In going there I developed a respect and fondness for many of the Iraqi people, which I didn't have when I first arrived. On the contrary, when I first got to Iraq I viewed them as a defeated enemy worthy of nothing more than my disdain and contempt. The richness of their culture and history was unknown to me. I did not understand that it could rightly be considered the historical birthplace of civilization, with a rich culture and good and decent people. None of that was known to me, nor really mattered to me before my arrival.

Once I got there, and once I got to know many of the Iraqis who touched my daily life, my opinion of them changed. Most who worked for the Americans risked their lives every day on our behalf, and did much to make our lives a little more bearable during our stay. I will always be indebted to those I worked closely with and got to know. Most of the Iraqis truly are a good, decent people. Thrust into a war not of their choosing and occupied by people from a strange and distant land, they did their best to try to understand us and in many cases tolerate our outrageous behavior.

There was a great deal of learning to be done on each of our parts, and the Iraqis I was privileged to get to know did so with dignity and a humbleness that endeared them to me and the others they worked with. What has happened to their country following the American involvement is truly sad. It is for others to argue and discuss the wisdom of the United States ever going into Iraq in the first place, but I will always treasure some of the relationships that developed between the American instructors and our Iraqi students, the translators and the others we came into contact with on a daily basis.

But mostly what I thought about while sitting there waiting for a ride home, was what I was going to do now. I suspected there was a good chance I had not seen the last of Baghdad, a suspicion that would prove justified—I would return several times for different jobs, spending a total of roughly three years on the ground in Iraq, almost all of it in the city of Baghdad.

.

CHAPTER 24

Thank You for Your Service

Missing among all the accolades and well-meaning expressions of thanks we received when we got home was the recognition that our loved ones went through as much or more than we experienced over in Baghdad. It's the same in any conflict any nation has ever been involved in. The men-folk up and leave, off to fight in wars and find glory, while the women-folk and children remain behind to take care of the home and to worry. Not enough credit is given to those who remain behind, never knowing what each day might bring for their loved ones serving in harm's way.

I truly believe it is easier for us over in the war zones because we at least know what's going on day in and day out. We're living it. We know what's happening around us, what the daily threats are. Our loved ones back home know only what they see in the news media, which as we all know can slant things to suit whatever their political or social agenda might be.

I remember one time in the Green Zone when I was walking across a couple of parking lots towards the military's PX, I noticed a news reporter standing in front of a cameraman, giving a 'live' report for a network to broadcast to the folks back home. The reporter was wearing his full 'battle rattle', Kevlar helmet and all. I stopped and watched briefly to see what was going on and heard the reporter say, "Reporting live with the 3rd ID in Tikrit." Well, the 3rd Infantry Division was indeed involved in a major operation in the area of Tikrit at the time, but this reporter was nowhere near them. He was safe and sound in the Green Zone in Baghdad, standing outside Saddam's Palace. I just shook my head and continued my stroll towards the PX.

I remember being overseas many years ago, when all we had was 'snail mail' and the occasional telephone call. I distinctly recall waiting for mail call every day, to see if there was a letter from back home. It was a regular ritual, checking your mailbox, only to walk away a little dejected when it was empty. My mother was a great letter writer, and I remember that she had wonderful handwriting, something that is becoming a lost art. Do they even teach cursive writing anymore? Mom would write long letters covering several pages, and she would try to bring me up-to-date on what was going on back in my hometown, and in the States as a whole. On a few occasions she would even send a cassette tape so that I could hear familiar voices.

But back in Baghdad in the year 2005 we had instant messaging, in addition to the small cell phones we all purchased and used to call home as often as we could (after factoring in the 10- or 12-hour time difference). I would instant message with loved ones as often as the spotty internet service allowed. I would try to tell everyone what was happening—naturally keeping OPSEC rules in mind. On a number of occasions I had to ask someone to hold on for a minute because mortar rounds had started impacting somewhere not far away, though I never told them that was the reason. I would crawl under my bunk and pull on my body armor and Kevlar helmet, not that any of it would have provided an ounce of protection if there was a direct hit on the Tin Hut. Actually, it would have put the hut out of its misery, but it wouldn't have done any of us inside at the time a bit of good. I'm sure everyone found such occasions a little disconcerting. Fortunately, I was always able to get back online fairly quickly and reassure everyone that all was well. Mortar attacks were usually short affairs.

But I know it had to be very difficult for those who only knew what they saw in the news, never knowing from one minute to the next how I was. I know my kids had their concerns, though by this time they had their own families to keep their minds occupied. So I want to say 'thank you' to Julie, my kids, and even to my ex-wife, Christina, who gave me three wonderful children. They all deserve my appreciation for hanging in there with me through this time. It couldn't have been easy for them.

And finally I just want to say, hey kids! Your dear old dad made it.

CHAPTER 25

Lessons Learned

My time at the Baghdad Police Academy taught me one important lesson about our nation's involvement in these types of training programs in developing nations overseas. The cream doesn't always rise to the top.

The so-called 'powers that be' sit comfortably in their cushy offices, 'harrumphing' with their arms folded across their chest, while others are out there taking the risks—basically doing the work that makes the leaders look good. Those on the ground, carrying the load, do all the heavy lifting. In Iraq (and the same term has probably been used in all wars), we referred to the Green Zone critters as REMs—Rear Echelon Motherfuckers. For the most part they didn't really give a damn about the people they were lording it over. Hence their favorite refrain for any criticism of them or the program: "Window or aisle." Yes, just bitching and whining can get old and isn't productive, but genuine concerns and criticisms, along with suggestions for improvement, should be encouraged. They weren't with the ICITAP program in Baghdad. They never really gave a damn about the people who were on the front lines.

Hopefully, our overseas police assistance efforts have improved since my time in Iraq, though I don't hold much hope. When you throw tons of money at a problem with little accountability, you usually attract the wrong kind of people and generally create even more problems, oftentimes much of them concealed. Listen to your people! Get out of your offices and away from the higher ranks and see what's really going on! And trust your people to do the work they're hired to do!

All I can say is that I left Baghdad with my head held high. I busted my ass to try to make life a little more bearable for the people I worked with, and I will always hold the memory of those times we spent together, huddled inside a concrete bunker, among the fondest I have. We truly were a band of brothers, feeling much the same emotions as the people in the military experience.

And, all these years later, my thoughts often drift, wondering how my brothers and sisters are doing and hoping, maybe one day, to see them all again.